Eating Forward™

*The New Way to Create Amazing
& Easy Family Dinners*

Sandi Richard

Bhessing Sandi :-)

Cooking for the Rushed Inc.

Published by Cooking for the Rushed Inc.
www.cookingfortherushed.com

COOKING FOR THE RUSHED™, EATING FORWARD™ and EAT SHEET™
are trademarks of Cooking for the Rushed Inc.

For information about special discounts for bulk purchases go to
www.cookingfortherushed.com

Library and Archives Canada Cataloguing in Publication

Richard, Sandi, 1959-
        Eating forward : the new way to create amazing & easy family dinners / Sandi Richard.

(Cooking for the rushed)
Includes index.
ISBN 978-0-9685226-6-0

        1. Nutrition. 2. Quick and easy cooking. I. Title. II. Series: Richard, Sandi, 1959- .
Cooking for the rushed.

TX833.5.R515 2010   641.5'63

Printed in Canada   Transcontinental Printing

10 9 8 7 6 5 4 3 2 1

To our readers and to our readers with diabetes
Eating Forward™ is not a cookbook which claims to cater to the complex dietary needs of a person with diabetes. The nature
of this book is speed and nutrition. A large number of North Americans have some form of diabetes; therefore we feel it is
helpful to provide information on food exchanges and food choice values.

In view of the complex nature of health in relation to food and activity, this book is not intended to replace professional or
medical advice. The authors and publisher expressly disclaim any responsibility for any liability, loss, or risk, personal or
otherwise, which is incurred as a consequence, directly or indirectly, of the use and application of any of the contents of this
book.

This book is dedicated to
**My Children and Grandaughter
Who Continue to Amaze & Inspire Me Daily**

Table of Contents

Green:	Mole Chicken with Rice and Broccoli
Yellow:	Calabrese Lasagna with Spinach Salad
Red:	Beef & Bok Choy on Vermicelli Pasta
Red:	Crispy Lemon Chicken (or Fish) with Rice and Snap Peas
Blue:	Raspberry-Maple Ribs, Sweet Potato Salad and Celery Sticks

Table of Contents

Table of Contents

Introduction:

Eating Forward™ Brings Freedom to Dinner

> **The hurdle we must overcome before our families can get healthy is time!**

I'll say it again—time is the hurdle, not food and not exercise! Food and exercise are just tools in our toolbox to get and stay healthy!

If food and exercise ARE the solution, why haven't we fixed our health problems? We keep trying to fix them with the same thing (food) in a different way, yet North Americans keep getting more and more unhealthy!

Overweight people are sick and tired of having everyone shove their diet plans down their throats and healthly weight people are sick and tired of hearing about how all kinds of government money and energy are going to people who are overweight.

> **We have to start thinking smart and stop thinking fat!**

We have to start thinking smart and stop thinking fat—there are a lot of unhealthy, skinny people out there. They just don't know they're unhealthy because we, as a society, have used fat as the ruler stick in which we decide whether someone is healthy or not!

In my book *The Healthy Family*, Gordon Matheson MD, PhD, Chief, Division of Sports Medicine Stanford University writes, "as of today Amazon stocks 26,418 books under diet and Google has 4.1 million websites on food!" That was back in 2003—now those numbers are: 56,239 books under diet and 6 million websites on food. If information on food was going to fix us, don't you think with all that information we would be fixed?

> **We have to take dinner off our overtaxed minds,**
> **because our minds are already so full of all the things we have to do.**
> **Dinner is too important to have on a to do list!**

You have a leak in your house. Water keeps dripping from the ceiling so you call the plumber. What if the plumber came to you and said, "I have the solution for your leak, I've turned the main water line off." You would look at the plumber as if he was nuts. "I need the main water line on." "Well," the plumber says, "if you turn the water back on your pipe will leak!" I'm sure you're thinking well that's just stupid…the plumber has to go to the root of the problem. He can't just turn the water off. We need the water. We will grow weary and frustrated unless the root of the problem is found.

By not fixing our dinner problem (and the problem is a society bombarded with too much to do) but instead offering stupid (I, I, I, I mean unrealistic) solutions with food; we are just driving people to the take-out joints…they're pooped—and they are soooo pooped they give up!

Instead, if we look at our lives each day, understand its busyness, know what we are eating in relation to that busyness and then head out for the day, we will have taken dinner off our minds. We will also be equipped with essential information as to how to eat in the day. Think about it…if you are having steak, potatoes and salad for dinner you won't feel like that at lunch. You, by sheer observation, will naturally balance what you're eating.

I personally love all kinds of foods. I love meat, fish, foul, veggies, fruit and grains.
But that may not be you! You may be vegetarian or maybe there is a vegetarian in the house. Maybe you are vegan. Maybe you have food allergies or just wish dinner could be pill form 'cause eating just doesn't mean that much to you. Whoever you are and however you eat—Eating Forward™ is today's solution to being healthy.

> **If you are like the majority of North Americans,**
> **you have no idea what you are having for dinner until dinner.**

If you are like the majority of North Americans, you have no idea what you are having for dinner until dinner. I have proven over and over again on my show *Fixing Dinner* that the worst of the worst suddenly feel the freedom of dinner once they know how. They are ALWAYS shocked by how easy it is!

Once they feel the freedom of knowing what they are having for dinner at the beginning of the day other areas of their lives seem to fall into place. It doesn't happen because they feel guilted into eating someone else's idea of healthy food! It happens because they begin to see how their old eating habits were a time issue, not a food issue at all.

Do you know what you are having for dinner tonight?

Eating Forward™ Is Freedom

I have chosen pizza for **dinner** tonight – my family will be so excited!

...therefore I will have vegetables and protein such as grilled chicken on spinach salad for **lunch**.

...therefore I should have a fruit smoothy or oatmeal with fruit and nuts or whole-wheat toast with light peanut butter for **breakfast**.

Normal food + knowing what you are eating for dinner = Eating Forward™

When you are Eating Forward™ you don't think about dinner all day, you don't hound anyone to help make that decision mid day – you are at peace. You feel great! There is emotional and physical balance! Instinctively you know how to eat during the course of the day, based on what you will eat at dinner. Everything is connected! Your body is in sync with your mind. Your mind is at ease, your sugars are balanced – you emotionally feel great about how you eat and how you feed your family. Your body has no need to store fat, it's happy; it knows you aren't throwing it a curve ball. You are emotionally in tune with dinner. It's a nurturing time for your body and for your family.

Now…What's typical?

North American's typical day:

Run out the door for work – nothing is taken out for dinner. Have no idea what you will be eating at dinner. Grab a coffee, and possibly a muffin, for **breakfast** on the way to work. Get the 10:00 A.M. sugar shakes. Eat whatever is convenient which is usually high starch processed food.

Get food from the most convenient source for **lunch**, either local fast food (let's say today you choose pizza), or something you have brought from home.

2ish in the afternoon – You likely phone your partner asking what they want for dinner or begin making a decision about what dinner is on your own, based on emotions and your evening schedule. If your partner doesn't answer appropriately, you feel frustrated and it may even affect your relationship negatively that evening.

Get home, to the new demands of the day – either make something convenient for **dinner** or maybe your partner ordered in, let's say...pizza, seeing the kids' schedule is full that night.

Do you see how dinner is actually an emotional and time problem – creating a food problem?

The North American's typical day leaves you constantly thinking about dinner all day long! Your mind is preoccupied. It feels like you've spent hours on dinner between thinking about it, asking about it, then having to cook it at the end of the day. It feels like it's taken hours out of your day – because it has!

How could you know how to balance your food during the day? It doesn't mean that it wouldn't balance accidently sometimes, it's just less likely because nothing is connected. My nephew, Dane, attends university and loves to cook. He challenged me on my theory saying, "Well I could do this exact thing the other way. I could choose my breakfast, then choose my lunch making sure I don't choose the same sorts of foods, then choose my dinner also making sure I balance dinner with what I already ate for breakfast and lunch." I explained, "Well that's fine if you're single and are really doing that! If you have the type of life where at the end of your day you can focus on food and nothing else…it can be done! Most people have a life where schedules are complex and there are other people involved, such as partners and children. It's very unlikely you will be able to block out life while managing to choose what you're eating, evaluating what you ate that day, and then cook dinner!!" My nephew got it!

> **You have no idea how deep rooted negative feelings can be when the "Asker of the meals" doesn't have a clue what dinner is going to be that night.**

What does the "Asker of the meals" mean? There is always one in every family situation. One person tends to take on the task of knowing what dinner will be each night. Soooo, because this person is already trying to be thoughtful enough to organize this, they are also thoughtful enough to ask other people in the family what they want to eat for dinner, especially their partner. This turns sour when the partner answers, "I don't know"! The "Asker of the meals" suddenly feels abandoned and the dinner task, strapped with emotion, feels larger than it actually is!

Eating Forward™ Steps

If you know you are having cheesy lasagna for dinner, will you want to eat that same thing for lunch? Instinctively you will choose something different. When you choose different foods your diet is balanced naturally. No counting, no stressing, no deprivation.

Diets, for the most part, are only sustainable for just a few weeks because diets do not incorporate life's busyness! When a person cannot sustain a diet, they beat themselves up and feel like a failure. By contrast, repeat the following steps for just a few weeks and life actually gets easier! This is because you now have three weeks of reuseable Eat Sheets™ that your family has created. No nagging, no fretting, no guilt. Just easy dinners your family has chosen.

Five Basic Steps to Change Dinner Time Forever

1. Go to www.eatingforward.com and print off a blank Eat Sheet™. Tack it in a central location in the kitchen. Use the Eat Sheet™ on page 14 as an example of how to set it up.

Tell your family members to give you dinner suggestions for meals they will actually eat.
You will likely need to ask over and over again. If necessary warn them, if they don't pick, you will. Believe me, it's worth the short term hassle.

2. At the top left of your Eat Sheet™ write down their meal suggestions and which recipe book they can be found in. Make sure the five meals are not all the same. You need a variety of meals to keep your week nutritionally balanced! If two people have chosen something similar ask someone to change their first pick, promising to transfer that meal to the following week.

3. Pour yourself a tea or a glass of red. **Find the five recipes the family has chosen and transfer every single ingredient from each recipe to the Eat Sheet™.** DO NOT LEAVE INGREDIENTS OFF THE LIST EVEN IF YOU HAVE THEM IN THE HOUSE. This is a reuseable Eat Sheet™, NOT THE LIST YOU WILL TAKE TO THE STORE. Write the ingredients under each category according to where you will find those items at your particular grocery store. Don't forget to include ingredients you serve with the main course, if the recipe doesn't include side dishes.

Put your Eat Sheet™ in a plastic sheet protector and put that in a small binder close to your recipe books. Show EVERYONE where it is so that Step 4 can be easily delegated.

4. Use your Eat Sheet™ to check which groceries you will need to purchase at the grocery store to complete your week of meals. The beauty of the Eat Sheet™ is that it is so complete. Anyone can use it to make a shopping list of the ingredients you will need to purchase for those meals on any given week!

Our readers tell us they create their shopping lists from the Eat Sheet™ in different ways. Some cross off items they don't need to purchase using a washable marker on the plastic sheet protector. Some use a separate piece of paper to jot down the items they need. Some go to www.eatingforward.com to create their Eat Sheet™ online, then cross off items they don't need to purchase (either online or after printing). Our **Eat Sheet Generator™** replaces step 3 if using my recipes.

5. Go buy your groceries! Then, every night at dinner discuss with your family which meal fits your schedule for the following night. Take out the stuff you'll need to defrost.

Each week you follow these steps you will add a new Eat Sheet™ to your binder.

On a week you just can't do this, use one that's already done.

**A shift in how I did things changed everything.
It gave me back my time, my health and family dinners.**

What we usually do is write down only what we need.

Grocery List

Amazing Chicken Stew
Tangy Slow Cooker Roast
Peanut Satay Chicken Kabobs
Macaroni Lasagna
Dijon Baked Chicken

Chicken breasts, boneless, skinless (7)
  (2 1/2 lbs or 1125 g) for 2 meals
Chicken thighs, boneless, skinless
  (1 3/4 lbs or 800 g)
Rump roast, fat trimmed (2-3 lbs)
Sour cream, no-fat (1/2 cup)
Garlic & herb seasoning, salt-free
Bottled peanut satay sauce (or Szechwan)
Soy sauce, reduced-sodium
1 can pasta sauce, tomato blend (24 fl oz or 680 mL)
Cranberry sauce, whole berry (3/4 cup)
Liquid honey
Strawberries (6)
Celery ribs (3)
Broccoli florets (1 lb or 450 g)
Baby spinach, pre-washed (12 oz or 340 g)
Multigrain buns (6-8)

This will only help you buy groceries on the week you make the list.
Your grocery needs will be different on a different week.

Eat Sheet™

RECIPE NAME	Page
Amazing Chicken Stew on Rice	114
Tangy Slow Cooker Roast, Potatoes, Peas	116
Peanut Satay Chicken Kabobs, Spinach Salad	118
Macaroni Lasagna, Veggies & Dip	120
Dijon Baked Chicken, Rice, Broccoli	122

MEATS
Chicken breasts, boneless, skinless (7)
  (2 1/2 lbs or 1125 g) for 2 meals
Chicken thighs, boneless, skinless
  (1 3/4 lbs or 800 g)
Rump roast, fat trimmed (2-3 lbs)
Ground beef, extra-lean (1 lb or 450 g)

DAIRY
Butter (optional)
Sour cream, no-fat (1/2 cup)
Cheddar cheese, light, shredded (2 cups)

PRODUCE
Onion (1)
Baby potatoes (20) or 4 large potatoes
Celery ribs (3)
Broccoli florets (1 lb or 450 g)
Precut veggies (1 1/2 lbs or 675 g)
  (e.g. celery, cauliflower, broccoli and carrots)
Mushrooms (12)
Baby spinach, pre-washed (12 oz or 340 g)
Strawberries (6)

DRY ESSENTIALS
Basmati or white rice (3 cups) for 2 meals
Macaroni, whole wheat (2 1/2 cups)
Croutons (1/2 cup) (optional for Salad)

BAKERY
Multigrain buns (6-8)

SPICES
Curry powder
Garlic & herb seasoning, salt-free
Hot chili flakes (optional)
Italian seasoning
Lemon pepper
Onion flakes
Table blend seasoning, salt-free
Pepper

BAKING GOODS
Cooking spray
Sesame seeds (optional for Chicken Kabobs)
Brown gravy mix, dry

HELPERS
Worcestershire sauce
Soy sauce, reduced-sodium
Bottled peanut satay sauce (or Szechwan)
Sambal Oelek (crushed chili paste)
Dijon mustard
Mayonnaise, light
1 can cream of chicken soup, reduced-sodium
  (10 fl oz or 284 mL)
1 can pasta sauce, tomato blend
  (24 fl oz or 680 mL)
Raspberry vinaigrette, low-fat
Cranberry sauce, whole berry (3/4 cup)
Liquid honey

FROZEN FOODS
Broccoli florets (3/4 lb or 340 g)
Baby carrots (1/2 lb or 225 g)
Baby peas (3 cups)

OTHER
Bamboo skewers (4-6)
Aluminum foil
Plastic wrap
Plastic resealable bag (1 large)

This goes into a plastic sheet protector and can be used to create a grocery list on any given week. Checking for groceries is a great job to delegate.

Time Saving Tip

Step 1   Become a member at www.eatingforward.com to access our new Eat Sheet Generator™

Step 2   Create your own customized Eat Sheets™ online from any of Sandi's recipes that you own

Step 3   Cross off items you don't need to purchase (either online or using a pen after printing)

Is the Diet Killing the Family Dinner?

What do parents do when they're dieting? How does this affect the family dinner?

> **If 85% of North Americans are already struggling with getting dinner on the table now, how do you think they are able to cope over time when they are faced with two dinners: one for them and one for the family!**

In the last 12 years of working with families, I have found that when parents end up adopting a temporary way of eating (food fad, diet, lifestyle…call it what you will) it usually only lasts around two to three weeks! Once life gets in the way…out goes the diet…buuut in the meantime while they are eating their odd diet food that doesn't take into account life, they are feeding their kids the very crap that got them to a diet in the first place—something convenient like take-out ooor something from a box. These habits are killing the family dinner!

> **When a parent is dieting, time becomes an even bigger problem! The parent has to figure out a way of eating to suit the diet and at the same time has to figure out what to feed the kids!**

We've already established that food is not the problem. It's time. When a parent is dieting, time becomes an even bigger problem! The parent has to figure out a way of eating to suit the diet and at the same time has to figure out what to feed the kids! This only adds to a parent's long list of to do's! In addition…the message a parent is sending to their child at dinner time is that there is no such thing as a family dinner. In other words, "Mommy has to eat special food because mommy thinks she's fat." We know statistically that this behavior can spiral the kids into having issues with food for a lifetime. How sad!!! It doesn't have to be this way!

Is the Diet Killing the Family Dinner? (cont.)

I want you to imagine you are at work. Your boss tells you he needs you to accomplish two tasks. The first is something you absolutely love doing! It's something that makes you feel fulfilled, special and joyful! It's a lot of work but at the end of it you feel satisfied, important and accomplished! The second task is something you hate doing. In addition, you still have to do everything in your job that you were doing before, while doing the task you hate as well! Then what if your boss told you that you could choose to do just one of those tasks full time. Let me guess which one you would choose!!! The one you hate—with all the stress and chaos of your regular job? Noooo, you are going to pick the one you love!

Now let's take that same example and apply it to dieting. Most people don't really want to diet, they just do it because they think they have to! (They may have to lose weight but they don't have to diet!) They think they can painfully go through the diet because it will bring them the reward of losing weight at the end. What actually happens is that the time and energy it takes away from LIFE causes so much anxiety that when it comes time to enjoy the reward, the joy is gone! They have received flack from their family and are just plain pooped trying to keep everyone happy, including him or herself! And then it gets worse…they fall off the diet! People don't realize that it wasn't a weakness in them that made them fall off the diet, in most cases it was life! On top of everything else, they feel like they've failed. They begin to feel resentment that their family didn't understand or support their dieting journey. Good feelings and good relationships in the home are crucial in today's busy lifestyle. So when we look deeper into the feelings and frustrations a person has when trying to diet, while handling a busy family at the same time, this can spell nothing but trouble for today's families. But, what if you enjoyed the process? What if the kids liked the food? How would the accomplishment of losing weight feel then?

> **Imagine waking up knowing what dinner will be that evening, you have reset your frame of mind to relax and enjoy your day. The stress of having to figure it out is "off your mind". The time issue is handled, so the anxiety is gone!**

When you can look forward to a delicious meal that will satisfy you aaaaand has a low calorie content, then the whole process of becoming healthy is something that you enjoy rather than dread! If on top of that it's easy to make and the kids love it, healthy is no longer about your body but the whole family's mental health as well, including yours. Now that's something to get excited about!!

500 Little Calories CAN Change Your World
…and Taste Great Too!

We've worked with real families on the go for over a decade now, so we know the number one priority for week day cooking is that dinner has to be easy to make and it has to be delicious! We get such a kick out of emails from people that say their family is healthier, they are more peaceful, relationships are better and that parents have lost weight. People are so surprised at these changes!

It's not surprising to us. We have worked hard, right from our first book, *Life's on Fire*, to make sure we kept our focus, no matter the food trends or fads, and have continued with the same criteria in each and every book.

Our first focus is that the whole family, including the kids, not only loves dinner but actually looks forward to it—this is huge! Our second focus is to make whole meals soooo easy to read and soooo easy to do that kids can get involved. A parent can assign age appropriate tasks and they should! Our next focus is to take the burden of choosing the meals off the person who normally does this! This is one reason we have never wavered when it comes to having full color photography for each dinner. It makes it so much easier for "the asker of the meals"! If I had a dollar for every publishing executive that tried to talk me out of the food photography to save on the publishing and printing costs, well, let's just say I'd have lots of dollars! But the fact is I know that kids, like adults, eat with their eyes. If family members pick a meal from a picture…they are more likely going to eat it. This alone will take a huge burden off "the asker of the meals." Finally, we focus on trying to keep most of our meals around 500 calories. So why is that soooo important in today's society?

If we assume a healthy recommended daily intake is 1500–2000 calories and you know you are having a 500 calorie dinner, you are left with 1000–1500 calories of flexibilty for your other meals and snacks. Dinner at home that is around 500 calories is vital in relation to how our society functions in todays world. Our lives have become so overcrowded with work, kids, activities and responsibilities. We are bound to have days where we are unable to pack something healthy for lunch. If you're eating out, the meal will more likely have a higher calorie count!

A Boy Named Steve:
Simple Changes, Big Results

A few years back, I was on a talk radio show that I was a frequent guest on. My favorite part about doing radio shows is connecting with the people who have followed my Eating Forward™ strategies with great success! On this particular show, I got a call from a young man named Steve.

Steve had heard me on this same show six months earlier. He said that listening to that interview powerfully changed his life. What really took heart for him was when I talked about diets. I said, "We forget that when we diet, almost all diets require you to drink water, reduce or eliminate alcohol and get lots of exercise. We don't even realize if the diet food isn't delicious and we fall off the diet, we turf all the components that go along with it!" In that same interview, I talked about the importance of energy balance and that if you are eating healthy food you actually like, drinking a lot of water and exercising, then you are bound to lose weight or maintain a healthy weight.

> **We forget that when we diet, almost all diets require you to drink water, reduce or eliminate alcohol and get lots of exercise. We don't even realize if the diet food isn't delicious and we fall off the diet, we turf all the components that go along with it!**

Like most of us, Steve loved food! All the different diets he had been on in the past had complicated eating plans or food he didn't like. Once he missed the great tasting food, like all of us, excuses started to flood in! Eventually he would drop the complicated diet food all together and along with it went the water and the exercise.

And that's what happens! People get sick of the food they are told to eat in order to lose weight. When they don't like the food, they drop everything else that was critical to the diet. Good bye water and good bye exercise, which means good bye diet!! Why is it that we only drink the water and do the exercise when connected to a so-called diet!?

Steve realized that he could sustain healthy living if he enjoyed the food! In the six months since first hearing me on the radio show, Steve lost 83 pounds! 83 pounds!!! The radio personality was blown out of the water! I was a little upset actually. I thought that 83 pounds was too much weight to lose in that amount of time! Steve insisted that he wasn't even trying!! He was just eating these delicious meals, started drinking more water and joined an exercise program at the local college…and the weight just kept falling off!

Then something really touching happened. It was at a book signing at a major bookstore and guess who showed up? Yep, Steve! He had Ron and I sobbing on the spot as he told us about his life's journey with food and diets!

He told us that growing up he was always known as "the fat boy" and was teased because of his weight. His parents tried every diet under the sun. In fact, his whole life was focused around a diet! As he struggled with his words and fought back the tears he said, "Do you have any idea what it feels like to walk into work these days, warm up food from last night's leftovers and have everyone want my food?" He went on to say, "No one wants the fat person's diet food! They can't believe I'm eating like this and looking so great! I never knew that healthy food could be deliciously mouth-watering. I had never experienced eating healthy food while looking forward to dinner each and every night! I didn't realize they could co-exist. I just needed to understand the energy balance (what goes in my mouth needs movement of some kind to burn it off)!"

I still get chills when I think about this event! (In fact, Steve…if you are reading this, you impacted my life's work more than you will ever know…but you will have to come to a book signing to hear my story!)

I don't like to talk about "diets" because I just don't believe in diets. I believe in something bigger than diets. Eating Forward™ means you can eat normal, healthy, delicious food. Eating Forward™ helps to make sure it fits your life. That's what dinner has to do…FIT YOUR LIFE! So next time you decide to go on a diet…you need to ask yourself…"Is this diet really about their food suggestions or about drinking water and moving your butt to get the results you want?" If they do suggest the latter, why not take Steve's lead…eat healthy, delicious food you look forward to and do the other stuff as well!

> **Eating Forward™ means you can eat normal, healthy, delicious food.**
> **Eating Forward™ helps to make sure it fits your life.**
> **That's what dinner has to do…FIT YOUR LIFE!**

The Value Menu Meal…Convenient or Costly?

On our Food Network show, *Fixing Dinner*, we work with different families to bring them together at dinner time. We also show them how to organize their cooking lives so that cooking dinner is do-able, affordable and easy for anyone in any circumstance!

One of the episodes featured four young, single people living in the same house. Two of them were students and two of them were working. All four of them ate pretty healthy growing up. In fact, one of those fellows was my son! Yep, Dan came to me one day and said, "Mom, the four of us need your help! We realize we are eating like crap but we don't have a lot of money and bad food is cheap!"

They wanted to eat healthy, but didn't want to spend a lot of money. "How can we eat healthy and still keep the cost down?" They estimated they were spending about $100 bucks per week on their meals and felt that that was pretty reasonable. I asked if they would mind gathering their receipts for their meal expenses. At the end of the week, I would come by and collect them. I went back to meet with them and told them they were right! Each person was spending about $100 per week for their meals. Doesn't sound too bad, right?

I asked what they were buying that was costing them so little! It turned out they were buying packaged foods and a lot of fast food meal deals. Most of their meals were around $5. I proposed that they adjust their thinking. Instead of being four single people living together, I wanted them to think of themselves as a family of four adults. Then I asked them to add up those receipts as one family. I explained to them that as a family of four, if each person is spending $100 a week, that's $400 a week which equates to $1600 a month on the so-called "cheap" food. The four of them just about fell over!!

Once each of them adjusted their thinking, they instantly realized that the cheap food wasn't cheap at all! Then came the hurdle…they couldn't even imagine how they would be able to adjust their schedules so that each one would cook once per week for everyone else. We looked at each person's schedule and organized meal tasks. One of the young fellows assumed it was impossible for him to cook because he worked late so he wouldn't get home in time to fix dinner. I said, "So after you get home from work and eat the meal someone else has made, prepare a slow cooker meal for the following night. Plan it on a night that doesn't interfere with other stuff you want to do!" Imagine getting home and having a meal all ready for you. You are going to feel better because you are coming home to their home cooked meal aaaand they will feel great when they eat your slow cooker meal the next night. It's a win win! They can put a plate aside for you of the meal you made, for when you get home, then the rest of the week you are off the hook! Each person ate heathly food all week yet was only responsible for making one meal. The fifth night we had them join forces and do a mixed grill on the BBQ which was something they usually did anyway.

I wanted to cut their expenses in half using the Eating Forward™ approach. But much to my surprise, when I arrived back at their home four weeks later, here's what had happened…their bills had dropped to a little over $100 per week for all four of them!! Their bills were a quarter of what they were originally spending!!!

> **These four became convinced that somehow they were tricked into thinking that the $5 meal was cheap. In fact, the $5 meals were extremely expensive, both on their health and on their pocket book!**

Another situation was a family that lived away from their extended family. They missed them desperately, but never seemed to have enough money to fly back home. They applied to be on my show because they wanted to leave their kids with the legacy of eating well! However, as we moved into the show, I saw we could also help them on the money front. I challenged them to dig up their receipts from the past month. I asked them to put into savings everything over and above what they used to spend vs what they spend when Eating Forward™. They were shocked! When I returned, they had already banked $600 for their trip home. (Remember, I went back 4 weeks after the show!)

How does this happen? In a nut shell, you go to the grocery store, buy groceries for one meal after work in a rush. The bill comes to 40 bucks. Your brain says, "If I ate out it would've only cost 20 bucks for the four of us." Sooooo, you think it costs more to buy the groceries. There are two factors your brain doesn't tell you. Number one; you're likely buying other things you need while purchasing the dinner ingredients like milk, bananas etc. Number two; you will have groceries left over, such as condiments or spices for the meals you will make later. When you purchase take-out, that's it, there is no food left in the cupboard!

> **When you purchase take-out, that's it, there is no food left in the cupboard!**

There are hundreds of stories I could share like these, but what I really want is for you to create your own story! Challenge yourself! Toss your grocery and eating out receipts into an envelope for a week. Then add up what you save using a tiny adjustment—Eating Forward™!

Everyone's a Food Expert
...No Wonder I'm Confused

What else is killing the family dinner? Everyone's a food expert!

I was shopping with Ron one day at a big box store. I got so excited when my favorite organic drink was available for a great price! I was getting my bill checked off by an employee at the door when she asked, "Are these drinks good?" I said, "Oh, yes! They are delicious and they are so healthy!" She looked at me and said…"But don't they have sugar in them?" She couldn't understand how a drink could be healthy if it had sugar in it. This immediately struck me. Yes, the drinks have naturally occurring sugar from the blend of healthy, organic juice. The nutrients far outweigh the small amount of sugar! Everyone has an opinion about what is healthy and what is not!

Our society is constantly bombarded with endless information on which diets work and what foods are healthy...EACH WEEK!!! We take that little bit of information and then not only make decisions based on something that we know very little about…we then go and advocate it too!

We've become trained to think that if sugar or fat or a carb or a starch or red meat…you get the picture…is an ingredient in the food, then it is not healthy, depending on who you're talking to! Just walk down the street and ask one person what healthy is and they might tell you that healthy means eating no carbohydrates and a lot of protein. Then ask a different person on that same street…they might tell you that you should only eat vegetables and grains to be healthy and never touch meat!

There are millions of diet books on the shelves with varying opinions. It's not that the science and learning about food isn't important…it is! But what's more important is what we do with that information! People who don't have time to read the whole book will take little pieces of information from someone else who thinks he or she is an expert. They then make a decision based on that person's experience. They try the diet for about 2 to 3 weeks, get fed up, start eating normal then move onto another diet based on yet another person's opinion. Meanwhile, we still don't know what "healthy" is!

I believe healthy is 1500 to 2000 calories a day that are packed with all kinds of different and essential nutrients. We have to make sure that we keep the information we hear in perspective. For example, if you are eating 3000 calories a day and are sitting at a computer station all day long then you are going to get fat! If you don't want to move your butt (which isn't a good decision), you will need to dramatically decrease your calorie intake! It's just that simple—quality food, energy in, energy out! But, if you are active during the day or have a laborious job then you will not only burn those extra calories, but you will actually need them to function.

I know someone who kills me every time he says, "I don't use recipes that have sugar in them!" This same person eats out…A LOT! In fact, I don't even try to convince him any more that what he is saying is ridiculous! He proclaims that he loves Thai and Vietnamese food. In fact, lemongrass chicken is one of his favorites. Well listen buddy, you go ahead and pretend there is no sugar in the restaurant version! Oh by the way, I have some ocean front property for you at a bargain in the middle of the Sahara!! Here's what's really scary…he is a health professional!

People go to a restaurant and have no idea what the sugar, fat or salt content is in the meals they're eating. But if we read these ingredients on a label or see them in a recipe we are aghast!

We have become a nation spoiled by convenience foods, yet we are immersed in food information! It's begun clouding our minds and creating an attitude that "if it's not in the pantry, we don't count it!"

Eating Forward™ is about knowing what you are having for dinner up front so that you can naturally know how to eat during the day! I am not here to dictate what "healthy" is for anyone, so don't email me if you've lost 3 rungs on your belt cause you ate only MYJIE soup for 1 week…or anything else! But what I do want to say is that we are constantly being fed information on what healthy means. We'll go for weeks without eating carbohydrates and then 3 weeks later decide that it's better to eat a diet high in carbohydrates and low in fat. We are freaking our bodies out!!!! Eating Forward™ will help you to eat balanced! And…everyone needs to move their butt, go for a walk and drink water too, especially if you work at a computer all day!

Adjusting Nutritional Data
To Your Specific Needs

Before we get to the fun stuff in the upcoming pages, we need to deal with a few details. It's only one page and you don't need to read it like the rest of the book, but can tag it if you want it readily available for easy reference.

- Most of the recipes in Eating Forward™ provide 4-6 servings.
- Our test families varied in size. Some families said there was too much food for 4 people and others thought it was just right.
- If you have 4 adults in your home with very healthy appetites the meal will probably serve 4 (when we write Serves 4-6). Sometimes someone gets a left-over lunch the next day!
- If you have younger children the recipe will probably serve 6 (when we write Serves 4-6).
- When a range is given for the number of servings a meal makes, the higher number is used.
  (i.e. When a meal says 4-6 servings, the nutritional data assumes you are dividing every component of the entire meal into 6 portions. The nutritional data is for one portion of each component. This also applies to the food exchange and food group data.)
  Use the formula below to adjust the nutritional data when we write "Serves 4-6" and for your family it serves 4.

Adjusting Data when a Meal Serves 4 instead of 6

of g fat x 1.5 = # of g fat
i.e. 12 g fat x 1.5 = 18 g fat
(12 g fat per serving for 6 servings) = (18 g fat per serving for 4 servings)

This formula works for all our nutritional data.

Weights and Measures

- Imperial and Metric conversions are approximate only.
- Occasionally we do not provide exact conversions so readers can identify with the can, jar and package sizes produced in their country.
- When more than one unit of measure is provided, nutritional data is calculated using the first named.
- When a range is given for a measure, the first given is used to calculate nutritional data.
- When a choice of two ingredients are listed (i.e. chicken or pork), the first is used for nutritional data.
- Ingredients listed as "optional" are not included in nutritional data.
- Fresh garlic (from a jar) is packed in citric acid (not oil).
- Vegetables and fruits are medium size unless otherwise specified.
- Buns are 1 1/2 oz (or 45 g).
- When using cooking spray, we assume a 2 second spray.
- **Our meals most often adhere to the following guidelines for the complete dinner:**
  Calories: 350-500 calories/serving; **Fat**: less than 25 g/serving; **Carbohydrates**: 30-70 g/serving; **Protein**: 25-35 g/serving; **Sodium**: less than 1000 mg/serving
  Calories from fat should not exceed 30% of your total caloric intake each day.

Diabetic Food Exchanges and Food Choices

A very large number of people have some form of diabetes, so we feel it is important to include this information as well as the detailed nutritional analysis. Our recipes have very high standards for taste, speed and nutrition. It seems only fair to allow a person with diabetes the luxury of being able to use a regular cookbook with great-tasting meals. They can simply adjust components according to their specific dietary requirements. There is another very important reason for having food exchanges or choices. Some people use food exchanges or choices as a tool to monitor their eating habits for maintaining a healthy weight.

The Canadian Diabetes Association (www.diabetes.ca) and the American Diabetes Association (www.diabetes.org) have revised their meal planning systems since 2004. The Canadian meal planning guide (Beyond the Basics) and the American meal planning guide (Diabetes Food Pyramid) describe common food groups (starch, fruit, dairy and other carbs) based on the carbohydrate content (in grams) of specific portion sizes.

Using these systems or the American Diabetes Association Exchange System and aiming for a consistant intake of carbohydrate as part of a well balanced diet helps in the maintenance of healthy blood glucose levels. One carbohydrate choice is 15 g of carbohydrate. Non-starchy vegetables contain very little carbohydrate.

The Nutrition Facts tables on food packages assist consumers to calculate the carbohydrate, sodium and fat in their meals.

Visit **www.diabetes.ca** for information and resources from the **Canadian Diabetes Association**'s website.

Visit **www.diabetes.org** for the exchange list, the pyramid, information, and resources from the **American Diabetes Association**'s website.

Equipment List:	Per serving:		
BBQ or broiler pan	Calories	328	
BBQ tongs	Fat	7.8 g	
Large stove-top pot	Protein	26.5 g	
Small stove-top pot	Carbohydrate	39.0 g	
Cutting board	Fiber	4.9 g	
Colander	Sodium	94 mg	
Medium serving bowl			
Sharp veggie knife			
2 stirring spoons	U.S. Food		Cdn. Food
Fork	Exchanges:		Choices:
Measuring cups and spoons	2 Starch		2 1/2 Carb
Aluminum foil	3 Meat-lean	3	Meat/Alt
	1 Vegetable		

Canada's Choices and America's Exchanges are included for each meal in our book.

Nutritional data, including food choices and exchanges, are calculated for the entire meal (per serving).

Sodium content is included for the benefit of those monitoring salt intake.

Why Should I Buy That Ingredient?
What the Heck Will I Use it for Again?

DRY

Spices you don't normally purchase- can really make a difference in a recipe. Store in a dark cupboard, they last a reeeally long time!

Black-eyed peas, chickpeas or lentils- you can buy just what you need in most bulk sections.

Sesame seeds- they make almost anything look great! Toasted sesame seeds have more absorbable calcium so either buy them toasted or make sure they are being toasted, which they are if you are baking them on top of something.

Panko flakes- are dry, fine, white Japanese bread crumbs. They really make a difference in crunchy coatings! They are easy to find at your grocer in the coating mix aisle. I used to have to go to an Asian market to get them…either way it's worth it once you try them…you'll see! I use them a few times in this book!

SAUCES, PASTES, SWEETENERS & FLAVORINGS

Salsa- can be added to almost any sauce for flavor and texture. Stores great in the fridge long term, less if it's home made.

Pesto- amazing as a pizza base instead of tomato sauce. Fabulous to dab on grilling veggies. Keeps fairly long term in fridge (but once you start seeing how versatile it is it won't last!).

Dubonnet- (sweet red aperitif wine found in liquor store) this is the greatest thing to have around for any recipe calling for sherry, port or marsala wine. It's about 10 bucks, you don't need much and it lasts forever in your pantry. Remember, alcohol burns off when cooking so you don't need to worry about the kids. We use it several times in this book.

Dijon mustard- is great in any sauce to add a little kick without too much heat. It's also great on sandwiches!

Soy sauce- can add a salty flavor to many dishes. But like salt—not too much! It stores beautifully in the pantry long term!

Fish sauce- adds this unusual, interesting flavor to most Asian dishes. Stores long term in fridge.

Hot wing sauce- adds heat to BBQ sauce, ketchup or any other sauce for that matter. Keeps long term in the fridge.

Curry paste- is a great boost to any stir fry, sauce, gravy or reduction. This stores long term in the fridge once opened.

Tom Yum paste- is great to kick up heat in any dish, but I mostly use it in a soup with a water based broth (rather than a chicken or beef based broth). It adds a ton of flavor but also heat. This paste lasts long term in the fridge!

Sweet Thai chili sauce- I have had so many people tell me this one sauce has become a staple in their fridge now! It's great when you want to add a little sweetness but also heat to a dish. It's a forgiving heat with a lovely sweet flavor. I use this in Asian and Indian dishes. I also use it to bring down the heat, yet kick up the flavor, on chicken and wings. See my wings recipe, YUM!

Kepac Manis- (sweet soy sauce) This is an amazing condiment to add to any stir fry or Asian dish. If I had to pick between this or soy sauce, I would pick this as it's much more versatile. Stores long term.

Sambal Oelek- (hot chili sauce or garlic chili sauce) A pinch can bring a nice, spicy heat to any sauce. Keeps long term in the fridge.

Sweet hot mustard- use on sandwiches with ham or in any sauce or rub where you want a little sweetness and a touch of heat. Keeps long term in fridge.

Maple syrup- this is one of the most amazing natural sweeteners for sauces or dressings. Store in the fridge long term. It is expensive but it goes a long way and lasts a looong time...sooooo cheap in the long run!

Peanut butter- is a great substitute for recipes that require you to purée nuts for a recipe. It's a quick way to speed up and add complex flavor to Asian and Indian dishes.

Chocolate milk syrup- can really be a quick addition to mole (the sauce, not the animal) or any dish that adds the complex flavor of chocolate. It stores beautifully for a long time and is a great way to get milk into your kids.

CANS, JARS or CARTONS

Coconut milk- I use light. You can use this as a replacement for milk or cream in Asian and Indian dishes. Leftovers freeze well.

Hot pepper relish- fantastic added to anything you want to give texture or heat to. Add to mayonnaise for a hot tarter sauce. Fabulous on hot dogs! Stores long term in fridge.

Olives- are great as a pizza topping and even if you don't care for them much, they are wonderful to put out with a little oil and balsamic vinegar with bread. Looks like you fussed when you didn't. Store fairly long term in fridge.

Mint jelly- any recipe, sauce or reduction where you think mint might add a little twist. Anything with lamb for sure. On its own, amazing on crackers with creamy cheeses. Stores long term in fridge.

Chicken, Beef, or Veggie broth- canned, long term storage; tetra pacs, more economical but limited fridge life. Are fantastic to add to almost anything, purchase sodium reduced when possible! I keep an oil marker in my knife drawer and mark the date I open the tetra pac.

Why Should I Buy That Ingredient?
What the Heck Will I Use it for Again! (Cont.)

Vinegars- great for dressings, sauces and for dipping with oil of course. If your vinegar goes cloudy, don't throw it out…it's called "Mother" or "Mother of Vinegar"! This is the stuff chef's love!

OLIVE OIL, CANOLA OIL or VEGETABLE OIL

Olive oil is great for savory dishes as well as dressings, sautéing veggies, combining with balsamic vinegar for dipping bread, drizzling on cooked pasta so it doesn't stick while being stored…you name it! Bottom line is it's good for you and it should be your most commonly used oil. It stores reasonably well at room temp but like any oil if you don't use a lot, buy smaller quantities so it's always fresh. Canola and vegetable oil are great for any dish where you don't want added flavor.

NUT & SEED OILS

Oils such as peanut and sesame have a high smoke point and depending on the dish are great in American, Asian and Indian cuisine, store great in fridge long term. Sesame oil can be used as a flavoring in Asian dishes rather than just an oil to fry in as well.

FRESH

Garlic or ginger (from a jar or tube) are great to have on hand during the work week for those days like…you get in a traffic jam and have to help Johnny with his 12 hour school project but you only have 4 hours! I use them in the workweek all the time!

Cheese you wouldn't normally buy like cambozola, gorgonzola or blue cheese. I freeze these after use. It actually makes them easier to crumble next time…and crumbled cheese defrosts in minutes. Mascarpone is great to throw into any cream sauce for meat or pasta, a little at a time. Really adds a nice texture and richness. Also great in desserts like tiramisu. Ricotta cheese—anything you would use cottage cheese in, including smoothies.

Conversion Charts

All measures are not the same.
These are a great guide, variances are minimal.

Liquid Measure

1 oz	30 ml
2 oz	60 ml
3 oz	100 ml
4 oz	125 ml
5 oz	150 ml
6 oz	190 ml
8 oz	250 ml
10 oz (1/2 pint)	300 ml
16 oz (1/2 litre)	500 ml
20 oz (1 pint)	600 ml
1 3/4 pints (1 litre)	1000 ml

Dry Measures

Dry Measures	stand	exact
1 oz	30 g	(28.3)
4 oz (1/4 lb)	125 g	(113.4)
8 oz (1/2 lb)	250 g	(226.8)
12 oz (3/4 lb)	375 g	
16 oz (1 lb)	500 g	
32 oz (2 lbs)	1 kg	

Can and Jar Comparison

4.5 oz	127 ml
8 oz	227 ml
10 oz	284 ml
12 oz	341 ml
14 oz	398 ml
19 oz	540 ml
24.5 oz	700 ml

Oven Temperatures

	F	C	F	C	
	175 - 80		350 - 175		
	200 - 95		375 - 190		
	225 - 110		400 - 205		mod hot
very slow	250 - 120		425 - 220		
	275 - 140		450 - 230		hot
slow	300 - 150		475 - 240		
mod slow	325 - 160		500 - 260		very hot

Buying Meat or Produce

1/2 lb	225 g
1 lb	450 g
1 1/2 lbs	675 g
2 lbs	900 g
2 1/2 lbs	1125 g
3 lbs	1350 g

Measuring

Measuring	stand	exact
1/4 tsp	1.2 ml	
1/2 tsp	2.4 ml	
1 tsp	5 ml	(4.7)
1 Tbsp (3 tsp)	15 ml	(14.2)
1/4 cup (4 Tbsp)	55 ml	(56.8)
1/3 cup	75 ml	(75.6)
1/2 cup	125 ml	(113.7)
2/3 cup	150 ml	(151.2)
3/4 cup	175 ml	(170)
1 cup	250 ml	(227.3)
4 1/2 cups	1 litre (L)	(1022.9)

Monitoring Your Fat (for the day)

Percent	If You Eat...	Your Daily Fat Intake Should Be
	1500 calories	50 grams
30%	2000 calories	67 grams
	2500 calories	83 grams
	3000 calories	100 grams
	1500 calories	42 grams
25%	2000 calories	56 grams
	2500 calories	69 grams
	3000 calories	83 grams
	1500 calories	33 grams
20%	2000 calories	44 grams
	2500 calories	56 grams
	3000 calories	67 grams

You Must Own

BBQ Grill Pans

In many parts of the world, we think that grilling is only for the warm weather. I challenge people on this. Most climates don't get super cold or have heavy snow fall for more than 4 months per year MAX. That means there are 8 months left. If you have the right BBQ grill pans, you will find that a grill isn't just for grilling. Grill pans are so inexpensive to buy, but really expand the use of the grill so it can be used more like an oven.

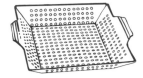

A grilling wok is essential for any stir-fry. It allows the stir-fry to have a smoky flavor.

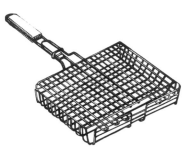

A grilling cage or fish cage is great to start with. I use this for veggie skewers, chicken wings (crunchy but not deep-fried) whole pieces of chicken, chops, fish, you name it. The beauty of it is that they are all in one basket so you only have one thing to flip.

A BBQ grill pizza pan is not only great for pizza, it works for fruit skewers, holding a roast for indirect heat cooking and a million other things, but I'm running out of room on this page.

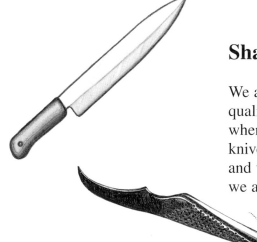

Sharp Knives

We all would love to be able to afford sharp knives of great quality. I slowly purchased mine one at a time and gulped when I paid the price! A temporary fix can be to buy knives that have sharpening holders. If you have dull meat and vegetable knives, it's one more excuse to give up, and we all know, we're looking for any excuse we can get!

Large Microwave-Safe Pot for Rice

Sometimes rice should be cooked on the stove, sometimes in the microwave and sometimes in the oven. It's all a matter of how the meal comes together and timing!

Salad Spinner

They are only a few bucks. Watch for a deal, it's an invaluable time saving investment.

Food Processor

All of our recipes do not require you to use electrical appliances other than a slow cooker, however, a food processor can really make your life easy sometimes and it washes up licky-split in the dishwasher.

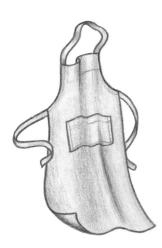

Apron & Timer

If you don't have an apron, buy one....a full length one. There is some strange relationship between changing into your jeans and not making dinner. If you really want work to end—end your work before you change!

The best investment I ever made for lowering stress at dinner time is an electronic timer. It's for timing you, not the food. When you time yourself during the work week there is a real beginning and more importantly a real end. I say to my family, "I've taken my stuff out and I'm setting the timer." My family knows that means DO NOT DISTURB.

Thermometers

An oven-safe thermometer can be inserted into food as soon as you start cooking it. It's most commonly used to cook roasts or game. There is nothing like opening up the oven and knowing immediately how my meat is coming along! These types of thermometers also have a guide for safe cooking temperatures. Even when you aren't using it, you can still refer to it when cooking something else.

An instant-read thermometer is one you insert into the center of the food once it's cooked. It gives you an instant temperature read. This type is for testing things like the internal temperature of a chicken breast or hamburger. The oven-safe thermometer can usually be purchased at a grocery store. You may need to purchase the instant-read at a kitchen shop. Be prepared to pay $20 for it. Once you own these and actually use them, your cooking, coincidentally, will have a much higher success rate.

How Do I Cook A Steak Perfectly?

Step 1

Let the steaks sit out at room temperature for at least a 1/2 hour before cooking. Why? Think of a pound of cold butter that's hard. The same pound of butter at room temperature is soft. Which one will you use to spread? If the oils in a steak have the chance to settle, the steak will cook more evenly. That may not be the most scientific way to describe it, but it's a description that makes sense to most people!

Step 2

Set your grill to medium heat (again, you have more control when the grill isn't set too high) and wait until it heats up. This takes about five minutes. Make your adjustments if using charcoal.

Step 3

Place your steaks on the grill. Give them a turn (not a flip) when they are easy to move and not before. Grill them for a few more minutes to ensure beautiful grill marks. Now you can flip and repeat the process on the other side.

Step 4

Take the steaks off the grill and wrap them in foil to rest <u>just</u> **before** the desired doneness. Meat continues to cook a little when resting. If the the oils in the steak are able to rest <u>after</u> the steak is cooked, the oils once again redistribute themselves through the piece of meat.

Steak Doneness Hand Test

Touch the end of your pointer finger to the end of your thumb, without exerting any pressure. Then take the pointer finger of your other hand and poke the large part of your palm just at the base of the thumb. It will feel really mushy. That's what a rare steak feels like when you use your tongs to squish the centre of the steak.

Now do the same thing, but bring a second finger against your thumb. Do you see how that same area has become firmer? That's what medium rare steak feels like.

Now do the same thing, but bring a third finger against your thumb. Firmer again! That's what medium steak feels like.

All four fingers against your thumb will be the firmest and that's what well done steak feels like! YUCK! I...I mean wonderful for some of you!

Prepping & Cutting For Speed

Forming a meatloaf for quick cooking

Score thickest part of your fish for even cooking

How to prepare fennel

remove ribs and root base

you can use the ribs to make home-made broths but they are pretty tough to eat, feathery parts make a nice garnish

Bottomless pastry pie in springform pan

A

B

C

D

Cutting for Speed

How to cut an onion

trim one end:

cut in half:

peel:

follow the grain to sliver:

cut again to dice:

HB

How to prepare asparagus

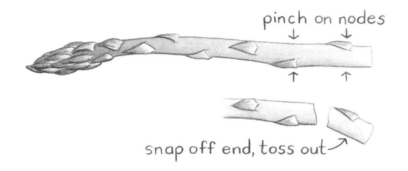

pinch on nodes

snap off end, toss out

How to cut a mushroom

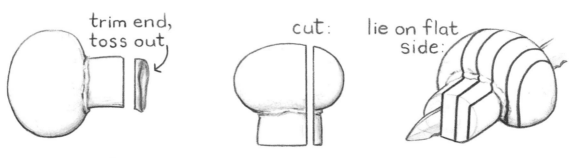

trim end, toss out

cut:

lie on flat side:

How to cut green onion

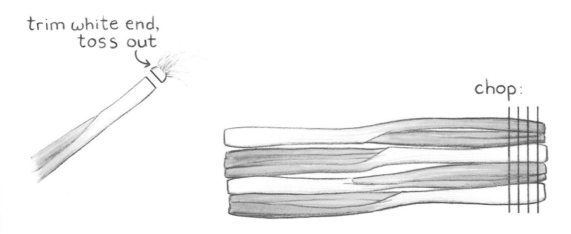

trim white end, toss out

chop:

Cutting for Speed

How to prepare lemongrass

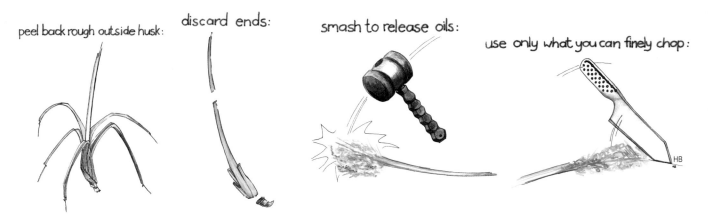

peel back rough outside husk:

discard ends:

smash to release oils:

use only what you can finely chop:

How to cut peppers

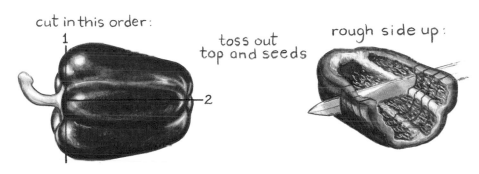

cut in this order:
1
2

toss out
top and seeds

rough side up:

How to butterfly chicken the easy way

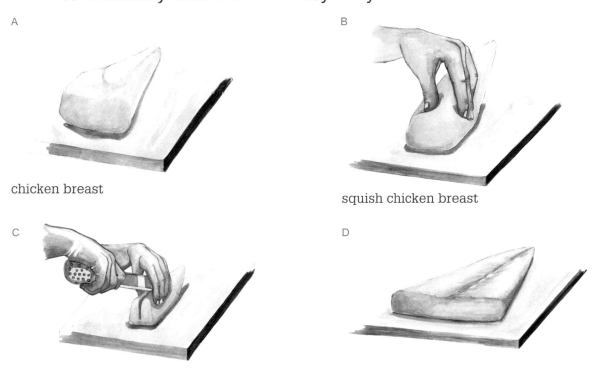

A

chicken breast

B

squish chicken breast

C

slice in half, but not all the way through

D

open up

Food Guides

MyPyramid.gov
STEPS TO A HEALTHIER YOU

I believe, as I always have, that the Food Guides are right on track. The problem has been the people reading them!

Sooo…both the USDA Food Guide Pyramid and Canada's Food Guide can now be personalized to your needs by going to their websites.

Before, the guides didn't know how much exercise you got. They didn't know anything about you, so it was your responsibility to follow the guides according to your specific information. Now they do the thinking for you. You key in your information and they provide you with a plan customized to your needs. If you cut my plate into three parts, half would be veggies. The other half of the plate would be split between protein and grains. That's how the guide works for me. Why? Because I only manage to exercise three times a week, and the rest of the time I am standing at a kitchen counter or working at a computer. My daughter Paige, on the other hand, played college basketball and now coaches high school basketball while she's finishing her teacher's degree, so she needs a few more grains than I do because she is far more active.

We also have to look at the guide from a financial standpoint. When the kids were little I purchased far more things like pasta and bread because it was inexpensive and I had to make my dollar stretch. But, I was running from morning 'til night and as a sanity break had a brisk walk every morning, so I was able to burn off what I ate. You can't go heavy on bread and sweets if you're sitting at a computer all day, come home, then sit on the couch. If you do that, you'll get fat and you can't blame the guides.

Go to **www.mypyramid.gov** or **www.healthcanada.gc.ca/foodguide** and enjoy their new interactive approach to making your eating life easier to understand.

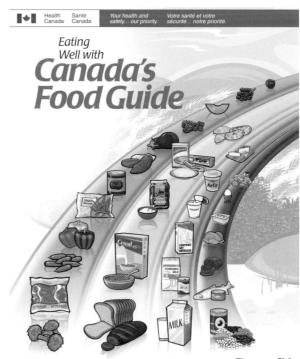

CANADA
healthcanada.gc.ca/foodguide

Look Before You Cook

Here is why you look at a recipe ahead of time. How many times have you started to prepare a meal only to find out the meat needed to be marinated for at least an hour? Get the picture? That's why visual triggers such as the Prep Code, crescent moon, slow cooker and BBQ are so helpful. These triggers will help you to match your meal to your schedule.

 **Prep Code** - see next page

A **Crescent Moon** above the recipe alerts you to a 5 or 10 minute prep the  night before so that the next day is ultra easy. Most of these can be started the same day, in the morning, if your schedule allows.

A **Slow Cooker** under the clock is a reminder you must prep the night before or the morning of your meal, using a Slow Cooker. The Slow Cooker fills you with wonderful feelings all day knowing that when you get home, your dinner is ready or almost ready.

A **BBQ Grill** under the clock lets you know at least one portion of  the meal is grilled. You may need to dig out a grilling pan if you don't own a BBQ grill. Grilling instructions are for a gas or propane grill. If you are using charcoals you will need to adjust.

I also include protein, carb and fruit-veggie symbols to the left of the instructions on each recipe. When you see a symbol - you'll know to shift to a different component of the whole dinner you are making.

 Red circle = some type of **protein**

 Blue square = some type of **carbohydrate**

 Green triangle = some type of **fruit or vegetable**

We named this icon **Carrot Top** (I know I'm a little looped in the brain). He helps people who want to eat less meat or are vegetarian. You can find him on the About the Recipes pages with directions telling you what to do to make the meal meatless. Take a look at page 40 and you will see what I mean.

Also...have fun with the rating page. Kids love getting involved and it makes your life easier when you want to choose meals at a later date. You will see what I mean on page 41.

Notice I never list weekly meals Monday through Friday. That's because I have no idea what your life is like each week. No one can tell you what type of meal you need on any given night except for you. You know who needs to go where, how much time you have or don't have and so on. Maybe you work Tuesday through Saturday.

The Prep Code

RED		YELLOW

and

Less Cutting and Chopping

More Cutting and Chopping

Dinner's ready in **30 minutes** or less
...when you need to get your butt out of the house fast.

GREEN		BLUE

and

Less Cutting and Chopping

More Cutting and Chopping

Dinner's ready in **60 minutes** or less
...when you have a small window of opportunity to prep,
but need to rush off somewhere while dinner is cooking,
or you want to relax before you eat.

About the Recipes

Green

This recipe was as much fun as it was a challenge. I wanted to use easy, family friendly ingredients like chocolate Quik without compromising an authentic flavor and of course with healthy data.

We made this vegetarian style by sautéing onions, mushrooms, zucchini and adding mixed beans such as black, garbanzo and black-eyed peas. We put this mixture on rice with the sauce over top! Really, really nice!

Yellow

Lasagna in the work week is a pain in the butt. This is not only easier the night you make it, but also provides you with a base for your cheeseburger soup and gives you an emergency back up meal…oh yea!

Vegetarians, use veggie grind.

Red

I loooove that our test families were over the moon that their families were eating bok choy and loving it! This has amazing flavor and is sooo simple!

This meal also turns out beautifully by frying pressed tofu in sesame oil until crunchy in place of sautéing your beef. Do everything else the same!

Red

Yum Yum Yum and just as nice with firm fish! If you are using a thin fish, reverse the order and make your sauce and rice first, then just heat up the sauce (you may need to add a little more water) when you're ready to serve.

Vegetarians can use the soy based chicken breast for this. Not my favorite, but popular amongst those who are used to the flavor.

Blue

These are my very favorite ribs. Remember, if you are away for more than seven hours it's best to start these after work for the next day. Most slow cooker recipes can't make it 10 hours without turning your meal into mush, even on low. I throw these into my slow cooker at high for 4 hours right when I get home from work, drain them and refrigerate. I'm ready to put them on the grill the next night as soon as I get home.

I always throw on a portabella mushroom stuffed with spinach, a ring of pineapple, red onion and pine nuts for my vegetarian friends when having ribs.

Week 1

Green: **Mole Chicken with Rice and Broccoli**

Our family rating: 10
Your family rating: _____

Yellow: **Calabrese Lasagna with Spinach Salad**

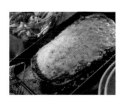

Our family rating: 10
Your family rating: _____

Red: **Beef and Bok Choy on Vermicelli Pasta**

Our family rating: 9.5
Your family rating: _____

Red: **Crispy Lemon Chicken (or Fish)
with Rice and Snap Peas**

Our family rating: 9
Your family rating: _____

Blue: **Raspberry-Maple Ribs, Sweet Potato Salad
and Celery Sticks**

Our family rating: 10
Your family rating: _____

Mole Chicken with Rice and Broccoli

Instructions:

Don't change yet! Take out equipment.

1. Heat oil in a large nonstick **fry pan** (electric or stove-top) at medium-high.
   Unravel chicken thighs and place smooth side down, swishing around in the hot oil. Leave until brown.

   Sliver onion and add to pan as you cut. Sprinkle with spice and garlic. Turn the chicken over with a fork and brown other side.

   Soften peanut butter in a medium size bowl in the **microwave** for approx 15-20 seconds.
   Add salsa, broth and chocolate syrup. Stir to combine. Pour over chicken.
   Simmer at medium-low, occasionally spooning sauce over chicken to cover.

2. Combine rice and water in a large **microwave** safe pot. Cover, cook at high for 8 minutes, then medium for 8 minutes. Place a paper towel under pot for any spills.

3. Rinse broccoli in colander or steamer basket. Place a small amount of water in the bottom of a **stove-top** pot and bring to a full boil with the broccoli in the basket above. Cover and set timer for 3 minutes...or microwave at high for 3 minutes.

   Serve Mole Chicken on hot rice. This is soooo amazing! Toasted sesame seeds on top add a nice flavor and look great!

Ingredients:

Take out ingredients.
1 tsp olive oil, extra-virgin

10-12 chicken thighs, boneless, skinless (1 3/4 lbs or 800 g)

1/2 onion
1/2 tsp cinnamon
1/2 tsp coriander
1/2 tsp cumin, ground
2-3 tsp fresh garlic (from a jar)
   (or use cloves)

1 Tbsp peanut butter, light
   (or almond butter)
1 cup chunky salsa (mild, medium or hot)
1 cup chicken broth, reduced-sodium
3 Tbsp chocolate syrup *(I use Quik)*

1 1/2 cups basmati rice
3 cups water
paper towel

1 lb or 450 g broccoli florets
water

1 Tbsp sesame seeds, toasted (optional)

Serves 4-6

DINNER IS READY IN 40 MINUTES

Equipment List:

Large nonstick fry pan
Large microwave-safe pot w/lid
Stove-top pot w/steamer basket
Colander
Medium size bowl
Cutting board
Sharp veggie knife
Stirring spoon
Fork
Measuring cups and spoons

Per serving:

Calories	422
Fat	9.3 g
Protein	33.9 g
Carbohydrate	50.5 g
Fiber	2.6 g
Sodium	535 mg

U.S. Food Exchanges:	Cdn. Food Choices:
2 1/2 Starch	2 1/2 Carb
4 Meat-very lean	5 Meat/Alt
2 Vegetable	1/2 Other

15 to prep

Calabrese Lasagna with Spinach Salad

Instructions:

Don't change yet! Take out equipment.

1. Preheat **oven** to 425° F.
   Heat oil in a large **stove-top** pot. Finely chop onion, adding to pot as you cut. Add garlic and stir. Finely chop green pepper and add to pot. Add ground beef, stirring occasionally until meat is no longer pink. Wash and slice mushrooms, adding to pot as you cut. Add sauce and stir. Cook until heated through, then **remove from heat**.

   IMPORTANT: **Set aside three cups of the sauce for Cheeseburger Soup meal on page 122 before making your lasagna.** *Sauce freezes beautifully.*

2. Slice bread lengthwise, remove most of the white bread from the center of each side with your fingers (about a third of the loaf). *I dry it out for breadcrumbs instead of discarding it.*

3. Smear sauce on the bottom of each side. Scatter cottage cheese on top of each. Sprinkle with Parmesan cheese and mozzarella. **Repeat layering.** Place one side on a cookie sheet. Place in preheated **oven** cheese side up. Set timer for 15 minutes.

   You will only eat one side. Wrap the other side in foil then plastic and freeze for an emergency dinner another time.

   ...while lasagna is cooking...

4. Rinse spinach in salad spinner. Sliver red onion. Wash and slice pepper. Divide spinach on serving plates and top with nuts, blueberries, feta, red onion and red pepper. Drizzle with your favorite dressing.

   Slice the Calabrese Lasagna into thick slices and serve alongside the salad.

Ingredients:

Take out ingredients.

SAUCE FOR 3 DINNERS
1 tsp olive oil, extra-virgin
1 onion
2 tsp fresh garlic (from a jar)
1/4 green bell pepper
1 lb or 450 g ground beef, extra-lean
10 mushrooms
2 cans tomato pasta sauce
 (24 fl oz or 680 mL each)
I use a spicy blend. Choose a low-sodium brand to reduce your sodium intake.

1 loaf Calabrese bread
(or crusty French loaf)

2 cups sauce per side, each layer has 1 cup
 (4 cups total for both sides)
1 cup 1% cottage cheese, per side,
 each layer has 1/2 cup (2 cups total)
1/4 cup Parmesan cheese, light, grated per
 side, each layer is 2 Tbsp (1/2 cup total)
1 cup mozzarella, part-skim, shredded,
 per side, each layer has 1/2 cup
 (2 cups total)
aluminum foil
plastic wrap

6 oz or 170 g prewashed baby spinach
1/8 red onion (optional)
red bell pepper (optional)
1 Tbsp matchstick almonds
1/4 cup wild blueberries, frozen
1/4 cup feta cheese, light, crumbled
 (optional)
1/4 cup salad dressing, fat-free

Serves 4

DINNER IS READY IN 25 MINUTES

Equipment List:

Large stove-top pot
Cutting board
Salad spinner
Cheese grater
Sharp veggie knife
Bread knife
Salad tongs
Can opener
Stirring spoon
Spoon
Measuring cups and spoons
Aluminum foil
Plastic wrap

Per serving:

Calories	427
Fat	14.9 g
Protein	30.8 g
Carbohydrate	40.3 g
Fiber	5.4 g
Sodium	1155 mg

U.S. Food Exchanges:		Cdn. Food Choices:	
2	Starch	2 1/2	Carb
4	Meat-lean	4 1/2	Meat/Alt
1/2	Fat	1/2	Fat
1/2	Fruit		

3 cups sauce and one side of prepared
Calabrese Lasagna is reserved for other meals.

20
to
prep

Beef and Bok Choy on Vermicelli Pasta

Instructions:

Don't change yet! Take out equipment.

1. Cut off the end of each bok choy at the root. Separate leaves and bathe in a large bowl of cold water to remove grit. Let stand.

2. Fill a large **stove-top** pot with water and bring to a boil for pasta.

3. Heat oil in a nonstick electric **fry pan** or large **stove-top** pot at medium-high.
   Cut beef into thin strips, against the grain, and gradually add to pan as you cut. Stir until browned. Transfer to plate.

   Add additional oil to the uncleaned pan at medium heat. Rinse and cut mushrooms into quarters adding to pan as you cut. Cut onion into chunks and add to pan. Sliver pepper, adding to pan as you cut. Add garlic. Add water, soy sauce, sweet chili sauce, Kepac Manis and stir. Slightly thicken then reduce heat to a simmer.

4. Place pasta in boiling water. Set timer according to package directions, approx 5 minutes.

5. Add precooked meat to sauce pan and stir. Add rinsed bok choy and toss with meat and sauce. Partly cover until bok choy is completely wilted.

   ...when timer rings for pasta...
6. Rinse pasta in colander and let drain. Return pasta to pot, cover, **no heat**. *I like to toss the pasta in a little olive oil while resting, it keeps it from clumping together.*

   Serve beef and bok choy on pasta. Make sure to drizzle sauce over top. If the bok choy looks like little celery sticks with green wilty tops, you have done it right!

Ingredients:

Take out ingredients.
6 baby bok choy (approx 1 lb or 450 g)
  (or 1 large cut into quarters)

water

1 tsp sesame oil

1 1/2 lbs or 675 g flank or skirt steak
  (or sirloin)

1 tsp sesame oil
8 mushrooms
1/2 onion
1/2 red bell pepper
1 tsp fresh garlic (from a jar)
1/4 cup water
1 Tbsp soy sauce, reduced-sodium
1 Tbsp sweet Thai chili sauce
2 Tbsp Kepac Manis (sweet soy sauce)
  (or use mushroom soy and honey)

12 oz or 340 g vermicelli pasta
  (use regular vermicelli or spaghettini, only use rice vermicelli if there are wheat allegeries in your family)

precooked meat
rinsed baby bok choy

1 tsp olive oil, extra-virgin (optional)

We usually serve this in individual pasta bowls for everyday. We love hot chili flakes for a spicy touch!

<u>Serves 4-6</u>

DINNER IS READY IN 25 MINUTES

Equipment List:

Nonstick electric fry pan
  (or stove-top pot)
Large stove-top pot w/lid
Colander
Large size bowl
2 cutting boards
Sharp meat knife
Sharp veggie knife
Plate
2 large stirring spoons
Measuring cups and spoons

Per serving:

Calories	425
Fat	8.2 g
Protein	31.7 g
Carbohydrate	55.2 g
Fiber	1.5 g
Sodium	322 mg

U.S. Food Exchanges:		Cdn. Food Choices:	
3	Starch	3	Carb
3 1/2	Meat	4 1/2	Meat/Alt
1	Vegetable	1/2	Other
1/2	Other		

15 to prep

Crispy Lemon Chicken (or Fish) with Rice and Snap Peas

Instructions:

Don't change yet! Take out equipment.

1. Preheat **oven** to 450° F. Pour oil onto a cookie sheet or large cake pan with sides. When **oven** is completely preheated, put oiled pan in oven for only a few minutes, then **remove**. Pour panko flakes onto a large sheet of waxed paper and place egg white in a wide bottom bowl. Dunk chicken into egg white, then press into panko flakes. Season with pepper. Place coated cutlets on the pan in the hot oil. Swish them around to make sure oil is underneath each coated cutlet. Return to **oven**. Set timer for 20 minutes.

2. Combine rice and water in a large microwave-safe pot with lid. **Microwave** at high 8 for minutes, then medium for 8 minutes. Place a paper towel under pot for any spills. Let stand.

3. Combine cornstarch and sugar in a small **stove-top** pot. Gradually whisk in chicken broth and lemon juice. Place on medium heat stirring constantly until sauce becomes clear. **Remove from heat.**
   ...when timer rings for chicken...
   Flip chicken over and reset timer for 5 minutes or until internal temp is 170° F.

   ...meanwhile...

4. Rinse snap peas in a colander and place in serving bowl on table. *These can be munched on before dinner or served with dinner as shown. Remember...kids eat more veggies if they eat them before dinner!*

5. Just before timer rings for chicken, reheat lemon sauce. You may need to add a little water. It should be thick but runny, just like your favorite Chinese restaurant. *This meal will be a hit for the whole family. Make sure the chicken is a nice golden brown color before flipping. Serve brown side up. YUM!*

Ingredients:

Take out ingredients.
1 Tbsp canola oil

1 cup panko flakes (found in coating mix aisle—or fine bread crumbs—but panko is best) *You will have some left over but you need that quantity for coating.*
waxed paper
1 egg white
4 chicken cutlets (1 1/2 lbs or 675 g)
 (or butterflied chicken breasts as shown) See page 35 for how to butterfly chicken. If you are butterflying the chicken yourself, give yourself a few extra minutes.
1/4 tsp fresh ground pepper

1 1/2 cups mixed rice
 I use Canoe brand with dehydrated veggies.
3 cups water
paper towel

1 Tbsp cornstarch
1/4 cup sugar
1/2 cup chicken broth, reduced-sodium
1/4 cup lemon juice
 Bottled lemon juice or from 1 lemon.

1 lb or 450 g snap peas
 If you prefer a hot veggie with your dinner, I love to toss my snap peas with 1 tsp of sesame oil in a nonstick stove-top pan. I toss them and just heat through right before serving dinner. YUM, YUM!

water (optional)

<u>Serves 4-6</u>

DINNER IS READY IN 30 MINUTES

Equipment List:

Large microwave-safe pot w/lid
Cookie sheet or large cake-pan
 w/sides
Small stove-top pot
Bowl w/wide-bottom
Serving bowl
Colander
Flipper
Whisk
Instant read thermometer
Small serving spoon
Measuring cups and spoons
Waxed paper
Paper towel

Per serving:

Calories	448
Fat	4.6 g
Protein	35 g
Carbohydrate	65.7 g
Fiber	3.6 g
Sodium	179 mg

U.S. Food Exchanges:		Cdn. Food Choices:	
3 1/2	Starch	3	Carb
4 1/2	Meat-very lean	5	Meat/Alt
1	Vegetable	1 1/2	Other

15
to
prep

Raspberry-Maple Ribs, Sweet Potato Salad and Celery Sticks

Instructions:

...the night before or in the morning...

1. Cut ribs into slabs and place them upright in crock of **slow cooker** as you cut. Sprinkle onion flakes on top. Cover crock and place in **fridge** overnight.
   Combine ketchup, raspberry jam, salsa, maple syrup and Liquid Smoke together in a small bowl. Stir well and store in **fridge**.

...in the morning...

2. Return crock to slow cooker. Add water to completely cover ribs. Cover with lid and set on **low heat**. If gone over 8 hours, see note.

...when you arrive home...

3. Preheat **BBQ grill** or broiler to medium (approx 375° F). Drain ribs in colander.
   Cut sweet potato into quarters. Smear oil all over sweet potato. Place in BBQ and bake until it can be pierced with a knife, approx 10-15 minutes. Keep checking as you want the potato firm. Remove and cool.

4. Brush oil onto membrane side of ribs and place on **BBQ grill**, oil side down. Brush BBQ sauce over top of ribs. **Reduce heat** to medium-low and grill for 5 minutes. Flip ribs, brush other side with sauce, and grill for 5 minutes. Flip one more time, brush with remaining sauce, and grill again for 5 minutes. Remove from grill and wrap in foil to rest and keep warm.

...while ribs are resting...

5. Wash, trim and finely chop green onion, celery and red pepper, adding to a medium size mixing bowl as you cut. Cut cooled sweet potato into chunks, adding to mixing bowl. Whisk together mayonnaise, sugar, vinegar and milk in a mug to make dressing. Drizzle dressing into sweet potato bowl and mix gently until well coated. **Refrigerate** until ready to serve.

6. Cut celery into sticks before serving.

Ingredients:

Take out ingredients.
2 1/2 lbs or 1125 g lean pork ribs, back or side (can double the amount to have extras)
3 Tbsp onion flakes
BBQ Sauce
1 cup ketchup
2 Tbsp raspberry jam
2 Tbsp salsa (mild, medium or hot)
1 Tbsp maple syrup
1/2 tsp Liquid Smoke (found near sauces)
water

1 large sweet potato (1 1/2 to 2 lbs or 675 g to 900 g)
1/4 tsp olive oil, extra-virgin
NOTE: *This is a 7-8 hour slow cooker meal. If you are away from home for more than 8 hours throw the ribs into the slow cooker on high for 5 hours while you are doing other things the evening before.*

1-2 tsp olive oil, extra-virgin
premade BBQ sauce

aluminum foil

2 green onions
2 celery ribs
1/8 red bell pepper

Sweet Potato Dressing
1/4 cup mayonnaise, no fat or light
1 tsp sugar
2 tsp vinegar
2 Tbsp 1% milk

4 celery ribs (or precut sticks)
Serves 6

DINNER IS READY IN 45 MINUTES

Equipment List:

...the night before...

Slow cooker
Cutting board
Small mixing bowl
Sharp meat knife
Stirring spoon
Measuring cups and spoons

...when you arrive home...

BBQ grill or broiler pan
Colander & Cutting board
Medium mixing bowl
Coffee mug
Sharp veggie knife
Stirring spoon & Whisk
BBQ brush & BBQ tongs
Measuring cups and spoons
Aluminum foil

Per serving:

Calories	533
Fat	28.7 g
Protein	25.5 g
Carbohydrate	44.6 g
Fiber	5.2 g
Sodium	710 mg

U.S. Food Exchanges:		Cdn. Food Choices:	
2	Starch	2	Carb
3	Meat-high fat	4	Meat/Alt
3	Fat	3	Fat
1	Other	1	Other

Assumes 10% BBQ sauce is wasted.

About the Recipes

Green

This is our son Jeff's favourite take out. I thought—how hard can it be to make? It turns out not hard at all. Using a food processor does make this way better. It grinds the meat so fine that when baked and sliced it looks just like the meat that comes off the gyro. I actually make two at a time as it is fantastic lunch meat. The beef and chicken together are my favorite but you can do one or the other.

This does not work well with veggie grind! So for vegetarians, load your wrap with hummus and all the fixings.

Blue

I love these drumsticks! If you don't like poultry skin you can easily remove it by pulling it off with a paper towel. Most of the time I eat skinless poultry but one exception is drumsticks and these don't disappoint!

Red

Kids rated this soup really high! Parents can enjoy the fact their kids are eating veggies and loving them! I use Italian sausage because you can get the meat at any grocer and you can choose either mild, medium or hot (we like hot). Sooo its super versatile for your personal taste.

Vegetarians, add extra beans to yours. You are going to love this filling hearty meal!

Yellow

I think this is my new favorite pasta! I just say the name and my mouth starts watering! It tastes sooo creamy, but it's low in fat and packed with flavor.

Vegetarians can cut up veggie based chicken strips.

Yellow

I loved that families rated this salmon so high. We keep pushing for families to eat more salmon because it is so good for you. By making a little low-fat buffalo sauce with your salmon, you'll be hooked in no time. Why not?

This is great for vegetarians who eat fish.

Week 2

Green: Donair-ish Wraps with Fresh Veggies

Our family rating: 8.5
Your family rating: _____

Blue: Sticky Sesame Chicken Drumsticks, Chinese Rice and Broccoli

Our family rating: 9.5
Your family rating: _____

Red: Chili Macaroni Soup

Our family rating: 9
Your family rating: _____

Yellow: Chicken Caesar Pasta with Peas

Our family rating: 10
Your family rating: _____

Yellow: Buffalo Salmon on Rice Medley with Melon Blue Cheese Salad

Our family rating: 10
Your family rating: _____

Donair-ish Wraps with Fresh Veggies

Instructions:

Don't change yet! Take out equipment.

1. Preheat **oven** to 375° F.

2. Combine meat and spice in a large bowl. Mash with a potato masher for about 5 minutes. *Or even better - in a food processor for approx 3 minutes if you have one! (The mashing or processing is very important!)*

   Form meat into a long, wide loaf shape onto a broiler pan or a cookie sheet with rack. Make your loaf short in height (1 1/2"). *See page 33 for illustration.* Place in preheated **oven**. Set timer for 55 minutes (or until internal temp is 180° F).

   ...while meat is cooking...

3. Rinse cucumber, celery and pepper. Cut cucumber into rounds, celery into sticks and sliver pepper. Rinse broccoli and cut into bite size pieces. Rinse tomatoes. Serve with ranch dip.

4. Whisk together mayonnaise, milk, vinegar and sugar to make Donair Sauce. Set aside.

   Tear lettuce into bite-size pieces directly into salad spinner. Rinse and spin dry. Wash and cut tomatoes into small chunks. Sliver onion. Set aside.

5. Tightly wrap tortillas in foil. When the timer rings, take the meat out, **turn oven off**, and place wrapped tortillas in the oven until ready to serve.

6. To serve, slice meat into thin slices, and reheat in a **stove-top** fry pan (unless you have just pulled it out of the oven). Pile meat into warm wrap. Drizzle with Donair Sauce, Thai sauce, toppings and cheese. *YUUUMMMY!*

Ingredients:

Take out ingredients.

1/2 lb or 225 g ground beef, extra-lean
1/2 lb or 225 g ground turkey
2 tsp flour
1 1/2 tsp Italian seasoning
1/2 tsp garlic powder
1/2 tsp onion powder
1/2 tsp fresh ground pepper
1/4 tsp cayenne (optional but amazing)

<u>Fresh Veggies</u>
1/2 cucumber
2 celery ribs
1 red bell pepper
1/2 lb or 225 g broccoli florets
10 grape tomatoes
  or veggies as shown
ranch dressing, fat-free

<u>Donair Sauce</u>
2 Tbsp mayonnaise, light
1 Tbsp 1% milk
1/2 tsp vinegar
1 1/2 tsp sugar
<u>Toppings</u>
1 head green leaf lettuce
2 Roma tomatoes
1/2 red onion

6 flour, multigrain or corn tortillas, 8"
aluminum foil

sweet Thai chili sauce (optional)
1/2 cup cheddar cheese, light, shredded
<u>Serves 4-6</u>

DINNER IS READY IN 60 MINUTES

Equipment List:

Broiler pan
Stove-top fry pan
Large & Small mixing bowl
Salad spinner
Serving plate
Small serving bowl
Cheese grater
Cutting board
Sharp meat knife
Sharp veggie knife
Potato masher
Instant read thermometer
Whisk
Spoon
Measuring cups and spoons
Aluminum foil

Per serving:

Calories	368
Fat	12.3 g
Protein	21.1 g
Carbohydrate	44.4 g
Fiber	3.5 g
Sodium	607 mg

U.S. Food Exchanges:		Cdn. Food Choices:	
2 1/2	Starch	3	Carb
2 1/2	Meat-lean	3	Meat/Alt
1	Fat	1	Fat
1	Vegetable		

15 to prep

WEEK 2

Sticky Sesame Chicken Drumsticks, Chinese Rice and Broccoli

Instructions:

Don't change yet! Take out equipment.
1. Preheat **oven** to 400° F.

2. Place chicken drumsticks in a large lasagna or cake pan. *You can remove the skin if you want less fat, but I like this dish with the skin on.* Combine honey, fish sauce, soy sauce, Dubonnet and sesame oil in a small mixing bowl. Pour evenly over chicken. Sprinkle with sesame seeds.

   Bake in preheated **oven** uncovered. Set timer for 20 minutes. *Actual baking time for chicken will be about 36 minutes or until internal temp is 170° F. Always use an instant read thermometer to ensure the chicken is cooked through, they are only a few bucks and really help you to know when dinner is ready.*

3. Melt butter with oil at medium heat in a large nonstick **fry pan**. Finely cut onion, adding to pan as you cut. Slice celery, adding to pan as you cut. Rinse and slice mushrooms and add to pan. Sauté until translucent and slightly brown.

   Combine rice, water and soy sauce in a large microwave-safe pot or casserole dish with lid. Add the onion, celery and mushrooms. Place in **microwave** and let stand.

   …when timer rings for chicken, leave chicken in, this is just a reminder to cook your rice…
4. Microwave rice at high for 8 minutes, then medium for 8 minutes. Place a paper towel under pot for any spills.

   …meanwhile…
5. Rinse broccoli in colander or steamer basket. Place a small amount of water in the bottom of a **stove-top** pot and bring to a full boil with the broccoli in the basket above. Cover and set timer for 3 minutes…or microwave at high for 3 minutes. Toss with butter if you must.

Ingredients:

Take out ingredients.

10-12 chicken drumsticks (approx 2 lbs or 900 g)
1/4 cup liquid honey
1 tsp fish sauce
2 Tbsp soy sauce, reduced-sodium
1 Tbsp Dubonnet (sweet red wine found in liquor store) or use red wine and a pinch of sugar or use grape juice
1 tsp sesame oil
2 Tbsp sesame seeds

1 tsp butter
1 tsp olive oil, extra-virgin
2/3 cup onion (or 1/2 onion)
1 celery rib
3 mushrooms

1 1/2 cups basmati rice
3 cups water
1 tsp soy sauce, reduced-sodium (or use Bragg)

paper towel

1 lb or 450 g broccoli florets
water

butter (optional)
<u>**Serves 4-6**</u>

DINNER IS READY IN 45 MINUTES

Equipment List:

Large nonstick fry pan
Large lasagna or cake pan
Large microwave-safe pot w/lid
Stove-top pot w/steamer basket
Small mixing bowl
Cutting board
Sharp veggie knife
Stirring spoon
Instant read thermometer
Measuring cups and spoons

Per serving:

Calories	521
Fat	17.6 g
Protein	35.7 g
Carbohydrate	54.3 g
Fiber	1.9 g
Sodium	466 mg

U.S. Food Exchanges:		Cdn. Food Choices:	
3	Starch	2 1/2	Carb
4 1/2	Meat-lean	5	Meat/Alt
1	Fat	1/2	Fat
1	Other Carb	1	Other

20
to
prep

Chili Macaroni Soup

Instructions:

...the night before...
Take out equipment.
1. Form tiny meatballs, adding to a large nonstick **fry pan** at medium heat as you form. Finely chop onion and celery, adding to pan as you cut. Cook and stir for a few minutes, then place inside inner crock of **slow cooker**.

Add dry beans and lentils to uncleaned **fry pan**, cover with water. Bring to a full boil, then **reduce heat** to a high simmer. Set timer for 30 minutes.
...meanwhile...
Peel and cut sweet potato into small cubes, adding to inner crock as you cut. Cut pepper into small chunks and finely chop cilantro, adding to crock as you cut.
Add broth, tomatoes, drained beans and lentils to pot.
Add spice. Stir, cover and leave in **fridge** overnight.

...in the morning...
2. Return center pot, with cover, to the outside of slow cooker. Set on **low heat**.

...when you get home...
3. Fill a large **stove-top** pot with water and bring to a boil for pasta.

Place macaroni in boiling water. Set timer according to package directions for al dente pasta, approx 7 minutes.

...when timer rings for pasta...
Rinse in colander under hot water, return to pot, **no heat**. Toss with a little oil if you like. Serve pasta in the bottom of each bowl and pour hot soup over top.

Warm multigrain buns are definitely a feel good with this soup!

Ingredients:

Take out ingredients.
1/2 lb or 225 g Italian sausage meat (mild, medium or hot)
1 onion (see page 34 for how to cut an onion)
2 celery ribs

1/4 cup black-eyed peas
1/4 cup chickpeas
1/4 cup black beans
2 Tbsp orange lentils
2 Tbsp green lentils
1 large sweet potato (1 1/2 to 2 lbs or 675 to 900 g)
1/2 green bell pepper
cilantro, small handful (approx 1/4 cup)
3 1/2 - 4 cups vegetable broth, reduced-sodium
1 can diced tomatoes (28 fl oz or 796 mL)
1 tsp Italian seasoning
1 tsp garlic & herb seasoning, salt-free
1 tsp cumin, ground
1 Tbsp chili powder

2 cups macaroni pasta

olive oil, extra-virgin (optional)

multigrain buns (optional)
<u>Serves 4-6</u>

DINNER IS READY IN 25 MINUTES

Equipment List:

...the night before...
Slow cooker
Large nonstick fry pan
Cutting board
Sharp veggie knife
Stirring spoon
Vegetable peeler
Can opener
Measuring cups and spoons
...when you get home...
Large stove-top pot
Colander
Cutting board
Soup ladle
Measuring cups

Per serving:

Calories	445
Fat	14.6 g
Protein	18.4 g
Carbohydrate	62.0 g
Fiber	10.5 g
Sodium	981 mg

U.S. Food Exchanges:		Cdn. Food Choices:	
3	Starch	3	Carb
2	Meat-lean	2 1/2	Meat/Alt
1 1/2	Fat	1 1/2	Fat
2	Vegetable	1/2	Other

15 to prep

Chicken Caesar Pasta with Peas

Instructions:

Don't change yet! Take out equipment.

1. Fill a large **stove-top** pot with water and bring to a boil for pasta.

   ...meanwhile...

2. Heat oil in a large **stove-top** pot at medium. Cut chicken into small bite size pieces, adding to pot as you cut. Add spice. Toss until meat is no longer pink.
   Add cream cheese, dressing and milk. Stir until cheese is melted and ingredients are combined.
   You may need to stir in a little more milk at the end, you want this thick but a little runny.

3. Place pasta in boiling water, stir and cook uncovered. Set timer according to package directions, approx 5 minutes.

4. Place bacon in **microwave**. Set timer for 1 minute. Set aside on paper towel. Gently smash croutons with a mallet or kitchen hammer to create tiny croutons. Set aside.

5. Rinse peas in colander or steamer basket. Place a small amount of water in the bottom of a **stove-top** pot and bring to a full boil with the peas in the basket above. Cover and set timer for 2-3 minutes or microwave on high for 3-4 minutes, then let stand.

   ...when timer rings for pasta...

6. Rinse pasta under hot water in a colander. Let drain and return to pasta pot. Cover, **no heat**, and let stand. Slice and crumble bacon. Serve the pasta on a plate or pasta bowl with the sauce poured over top. Garnish with croutons, crumbled bacon and Parmesan cheese.

   Warning…This pasta is addicting! It's so creamy you would swear there was heavy cream in it!

Ingredients:

Take out ingredients.
water

1 tsp olive oil, extra-virgin
3 chicken breasts, boneless, skinless
 (1 lb or 450 g)
1 tsp original, all purpose seasoning,
 salt-free
5 1/3 oz or 83 g cream cheese, light
1/2 cup Caesar salad dressing, garlic
 lovers, light, gourmet, refrigerated
1 cup 1% milk

12 oz or 340 g vermicelli pasta
(use regular vermicelli or spaghettini, only use rice vermicelli if there are wheat allegeries in your family)

4 strips fully cooked bacon, low-sodium
(purchase this way)
paper towel
1/2 cup croutons

3 cups frozen baby peas
water
NOTE: *You can toss the peas into the sauce if you want, but we like the peas on the side.*

Parmesan cheese, light, grated
(optional but amazing)

Serves 4-6

DINNER IS READY IN 25 MINUTES

Equipment List:

2 large stove-top pots
Stove-top pot w/steamer basket
Colander
Plate
Cutting board
Sharp meat knife
Stirring spoon
Serving spoon
Mallet
Measuring cups and spoons
Paper towel

Per serving:

Calories	503
Fat	14.1 g
Protein	32.7 g
Carbohydrate	60.8 g
Fiber	3.2 g
Sodium	442 mg

U.S. Food Exchanges:		Cdn. Food Choices:	
3 1/2	Starch	4	Carb
4	Meat-lean	4 1/2	Meat/Alt
1/2	Fat		
1	Vegetable		

20 to prep

W E E K 2

Buffalo Salmon on Rice Medley
with Melon Blue Cheese Salad

Instructions:

Don't change yet! Take out equipment.

1. Whisk sour cream, Dijon mustard, hot sauce and cream together in microwave-safe bowl. Set aside.

2. Combine rice and water in a large microwave-safe pot with lid. **Microwave** at high for 8 minutes, then medium for 8 minutes. Place a paper towel under pot for any spills.

   …meanwhile…

3. Spray a large nonstick **fry pan** with cooking spray.
   Wash salmon under cold water, pat dry with paper towel and season one side. See NOTE. Sauté, spice side down, over medium-heat approx 2 minutes. Season, flip and sauté other side.
   Reduce heat to low, cover and let simmer for an additional 4-5 minutes or until internal temperature is 155° F. **Remove from heat.**

   …meanwhile…

4. Rinse salad greens under cold water in salad spinner and spin dry. Sliver onion. Wash and slice melon.
   Divide salad greens on serving plates and top with onion, melon and almonds. Crumble cheese over salad and finish with dressing.

5. Heat Buffalo Cream Sauce in **microwave** for 10 second intervals, whisking in between, until hot.

   Serve salmon on rice beside salad. Drizzle sauce over salmon.

Ingredients:

Take out ingredients.
Buffalo Cream Sauce
2 Tbsp sour cream, light
1 tsp Dijon mustard
1/4 cup hot wing sauce *I like Franks brand.*
3 Tbsp cream, 10%
   (you can use milk, it will be a bit runnier)

1 1/2 cups wild and white rice
   I love Canoe brand.
3 cups water
paper towel

cooking spray

1 1/2 lbs or 675 g salmon filets, boneless, skinless
paper towel
1/4 tsp original, all purpose seasoning, salt-free (per filet – 1 tsp total)
NOTE: If your salmon is very thick on one end, see page 33 for how to score.

6 oz or 170 g salad greens
1/8 red onion
1/4 cantaloupe melon
2 Tbsp matchstick or slivered almonds
2 Tbsp blue cheese or feta
1/4 cup balsamic salad dressing
   (recipe below or bottled)
   I make my own by shaking together 1 cup balsamic vinegar and 2/3 cup real maple syrup…it's non fat and tastes delicious! It stores in the fridge beautifully, just shake before using.

prepared Buffalo Cream Sauce

Serves 4-6

DINNER IS READY IN 25 MINUTES

Equipment List:

Large nonstick fry pan w/lid
Large microwave-safe pot w/lid
Small microwave-safe bowl
Cutting board
Salad spinner
Sharp veggie knife
Salad tongs
Flipper
Whisk
Measuring cups and spoons
Paper towel

Per serving:

Calories	355
Fat	7.8 g
Protein	28.7 g
Carbohydrate	41.7 g
Fiber	2.2 g
Sodium	404 mg

U.S. Food Exchanges:	Cdn. Food Choices:
2 1/2 Starch	2 1/2 Carb
3 1/2 Meat- very lean	4 Meat/Alt
1 Vegetable	1/2 Other

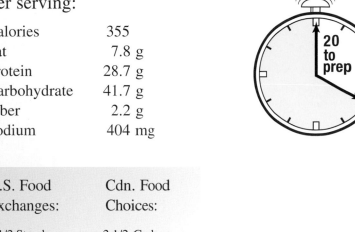

20
to
prep

WEEK 2

About the Recipes

Red

This is addicting and rated very high by our test families. They did point out that how much pork loin liquid you add back into the pulled pork depends on the size of your roast. Soooo start with less and keep adding according to your personal taste. We like pulled pork sloppy, some like it dryer. You pick!

Yellow

This is my favorite shrimp toss ever! It's so easy and loaded with flavor! Vegetarians can add pressed tofu in place of the shrimp (unless of course you are a vegetarian who likes fish).

Blue

My brother Neil gave me his favorite meat loaf recipe. I made it but cringed knowing how much fat there was in it! Sooooo as my dear friend Kathy puts it—"I fixed it." I love the flavor and our test families do too! Thanks Neil, but will you please eat my version—and live longer!
Vegetarians can make a sloppy version of this in a pan 'cause you know how hard it is for veggie grind to stay formed…but the sloppy version still has all the flavor!

Red

This is really delicious and was one of my most challenging recipes to get right with the test families. Thank goodness we got there! This is for one of those days you want a light meal. I just gotta have it with bread, I even like to dunk my bread in it! Yeah—bread and soup…you know!

Green

We did this chicken on a show with my crew from L.A. and you would swear they had never had chicken before in their lives! I am so lucky to have you guys! They swooned and licked their lips and so did our test families!

Week 3

3

Red:

Pulled Pork on a Bun
with Mexi-Mayo and Coleslaw

Our family rating: 9
Your family rating: _____

Yellow:

Shrimp (or Chicken) Toss
in a Coconut Broth on Vermicelli Pasta

Our family rating: 10
Your family rating: _____

Blue:

Neil's Cantina Meatloaf
with Red Potatoes and Veggies

Our family rating: 9
Your family rating: _____

Red:

Curried Butternut Squash Soup
with Spinach Salad

Our family rating: 8.5
Your family rating: _____

Green:

Peanut Butter and Honey Chicken,
Sweet Potato Fries and Snap Peas

Our family rating: 10
Your family rating: _____

Pulled Pork on a Bun
with Mexi-Mayo and Coleslaw

Instructions:

...the night before...
Take out equipment.
1. Heat oil in a large nonstick **fry pan** at medium-high. Sprinkle spice all over roast then brown on all sides to sear.

   Place browned roast inside center pot of **slow cooker**. Drizzle BBQ sauce all over. Pour water all around roast. Cover and leave in **fridge** overnight.

2. Combine mayonnaise and spice in a small bowl. Finely chop cilantro and add to bowl. Cover and set aside in **fridge**.

   ...in the morning...
3. Return covered center pot to the outside of **slow cooker**. Set at **low heat**.

   ...when you arrive home...
4. Preheat **oven** to 350° F.

5. Combine dressing and coleslaw mix with almonds in a large bowl. Stir until well combined. Set aside in **fridge**.

6. Transfer pork loin to cookie sheet with sides. Empty liquid from slow cooker into a large measuring cup or bowl.
   Hold pork in place with one fork while pulling pork down with another fork, creating long strands. Return strands to slow cooker as you pull. Skim fat off liquid and discard. Pour 2 cups of the liquid back into **slow cooker** over pulled pork. Add BBQ sauce. Stir gently to combine.

7. Place buns in preheated **oven,** then **turn oven off**.
   You can serve this as shown or the real southern way - with coleslaw, Mexi-Mayo and pulled pork on the bun.

Ingredients:

Take out ingredients.
1 tsp olive oil, extra-virgin
2 Tbsp chipotle seasoning, salt-free
1 Tbsp chili powder
1 tsp garlic powder
Pork loin roast, boneless, trimmed
  (2-3 lbs or 900-1350 g)
3/4 cup BBQ sauce
  (your favorite or see back flap)
2 cups water

Mexi-Mayo
1/2 cup mayonnaise, light
1 tsp chili powder
1 tsp cumin, ground
1/2 tsp garlic powder
1/2 tsp parsley, dried
1/8 tsp cayenne (or chipotle pepper)
Small bunch cilantro (approx 1/4 cup)
You will only use half of the Mexi-Mayo, use leftover for lunches.

1/2 cup coleslaw salad dressing
1 lb or 450 g fresh coleslaw mix
2 Tbsp matchstick almonds (optional but amazing)

2 cups pork loin liquid
  (1/2 to 2 cups depending on size of loin)
1/2 cup BBQ sauce

6 whole wheat buns

Serves 6
1/3 pulled pork is left over.

DINNER IS READY IN 25 MINUTES

Equipment List:

...the night before...
Slow cooker
Large nonstick fry pan
Small mixing bowl
Cutting board
Sharp veggie knife
Tongs
Spoon
Measuring cups and spoons

...in the morning...
Cookie sheet w/sides
Large mixing bowl
2 stirring spoons
2 forks
Bread knife
Measuring cups and spoons

Per serving:

Calories	517
Fat	20.7 g
Protein	30.3 g
Carbohydrate	57.8 g
Fiber	7.1 g
Sodium	915 mg

U.S. Food Exchanges:		Cdn. Food Choices:	
2	Starch	2 1/2	Carb
4	Meat	4	Meat/Alt
2	Fat	2	Fat
1	Vegetable	1	Other
1	Other		

1/2 Mexi-Mayo and 1/3 pork is left over.

Shrimp (or Chicken) Toss
in a Coconut Broth on Vermicelli Pasta

Instructions:

Don't change yet! Take out equipment.

1. Fill a large **stove-top** pot with water and bring to a boil for pasta.

2. Rinse shrimp in a colander under cold water and let stand at room temperature.

3. Heat oil in a large **stove-top** pot at medium. Rinse and slice mushrooms, adding to pot as you cut. Trim green onion then finely chop both white and green parts, adding to pot as you cut. *We like to reserve some of the green parts for garnish*. Add garlic.

   Rinse chili pepper, cut in half and discard all seeds. *Wash your hands thoroughly*. Finely chop, adding to pot as you cut. Rinse and cut red pepper into chunks. Rinse and slice zucchini in half, then in diagonal slices. Add to pot. Rinse lime and add zest to pot, using a fine grater.

   Add the following to pot in this order: ginger, turmeric, brown sugar, coconut milk, soy sauce, fish sauce and sweet Thai chili sauce. Stir to combine. Continue simmering while pasta is cooking.

   Fold shrimp or chicken into sauce to heat through just before pasta is ready.

   …meanwhile…

4. Place pasta in boiling water, stir and cook uncovered. Set timer according to package directions, approx 5 minutes.

   Serve pasta in the bottom of a bowl then ladle the broth, then veggies and shrimp on top.

Ingredients:

Take out ingredients.
water

1 lb or 450 g large shrimp, cooked, peeled and deveined (or cooked deli-roaster chicken) *If you want more protein, you may want to add more shrimp or tofu.*

1 tsp sesame oil
8 mushrooms *I prefer brown.*
1 bunch green onion (approx 7-8)
2 tsp fresh garlic (from a jar) (or 2 cloves)

1 small red chili pepper (optional)
1 red bell pepper
1 medium zucchini

zest from 1/2 lime

1/2 tsp ginger powder
1/4 tsp turmeric
2 tsp brown sugar
1 can coconut milk, light (14 fl oz or 400 mL)
1 Tbsp soy sauce, reduced-sodium
1 Tbsp fish sauce
2 Tbsp sweet Thai chili sauce

12 oz or 340 g vermicelli pasta (use regular vermicelli or spaghettini, only use rice vermicelli if there are wheat allegeries in your family)

Serves 4-6

DINNER IS READY IN 25 MINUTES

Equipment List:

2 large stove-top pots
2 colanders
Cutting board
Fine grater
Sharp veggie knife
Can opener
Ladle
Stirring spoon
Measuring cups and spoons

Per serving:

Calories	360
Fat	4.5 g
Protein	22.7 g
Carbohydrate	56.5 g
Fiber	1.8 g
Sodium	574 mg

U.S. Food Exchanges:		Cdn. Food Choices:	
3	Starch	3	Carb
3	Meat-lean	3	Meat/Alt
1/2	Other	1/2	Other

20 to prep

W E E K   3

Neil's Cantina Meatloaf
with Red Potatoes and Veggies

Instructions:

Don't change yet! Take out equipment.

1. Preheat **oven** to 375° F.
   Combine ground meat, onion flakes, spice, hot pepper relish, eggs, salsa, milk, breadcrumbs and shredded cheese together in a large bowl until well combined. *I use my hands…it's fun!*

   Form meat onto a broiler pan to look like a short, long, wide loaf—no higher than 2" in height. (See page 33 for an illustration of forming a meatloaf.)

   Spread BBQ sauce over top of meatloaf and place in preheated **oven**. Set timer for 50 minutes.

2. Wash potatoes and place in medium oven-safe pan. Toss with olive oil and spice. Place in preheated **oven** beside meatloaf.

3. Rinse stir-fry mix in a colander and place in a nonstick **fry pan**. Sprinkle with spice. Let stand.

   …when timer rings for meatloaf and potatoes, turn oven off…
   Heat veggies at high. Drizzle with olive oil and toss until heated through.

   …meanwhile…

4. We like to sprinkle extra cheddar on top of the meatloaf and broil for just a minute until melted. Watch carefully! Remove meatloaf to rest under foil.

   This is a healthier version of my brother Neil's best meatloaf ever. And now it won't give your body a fat shock, Neil!

Ingredients:

Take out ingredients.

2 lbs or 900 g ground beef, extra-lean (or ground turkey)
2 Tbsp onion flakes
1 Tbsp garlic and herb seasoning, salt-free
2 tsp hot pepper relish (or chopped up jalapeños) (optional)
2 eggs
3/4 cup salsa (mild, medium or hot)
1/2 cup 1% milk
1 1/2 cups breadcrumbs
1/2 cup cheddar cheese, light, shredded

1/4 cup bottled BBQ sauce (or see recipe on back flap)

20 red baby potatoes
1 tsp olive oil, extra-virgin
1/2 tsp original, all purpose seasoning, salt-free

4 cups stir-fry mixed vegetables (fresh or frozen) *Oooor… sliver red pepper, slice mushrooms and toss in snap peas.*
1/2 tsp garlic and herb seasoning, salt-free

1 tsp olive oil, extra-virgin

1/2 cup cheddar cheese, light, shredded (optional)
aluminum foil

Serves 6-8

DINNER IS READY IN 55 MINUTES

Equipment List:

Broiler pan
Medium nonstick fry pan
Medium oven-safe pan
Colander
Large mixing bowl
Cheese grater
2 mixing spoons
Measuring cups and spoons
Aluminum foil

Per serving:

Calories	489
Fat	16.6 g
Protein	32.3 g
Carbohydrate	52.3 g
Fiber	7.3 g
Sodium	524 mg

U.S. Food Exchanges:		Cdn. Food Choices:	
2 1/2	Starch	2 1/2	Carb
4	Meat-lean	4	Meat/Alt
1	Fat	1	Fat
1	Vegetable	1/2	Other

20 to prep

WEEK 3

Curried Butternut Squash Soup
with Spinach Salad

Instructions:

Don't change yet! Take out equipment.
1. Preheat **oven** to 350° F.

2. Wash potato and squash, then puncture each with a fork in several places. **Microwave** at high for 2 minutes to soften. **Remove** and let cool.

   …meanwhile…

3. Heat butter and oil in a large **stove-top** pot at medium.
   Finely chop onion, adding to pot as you cut.
   Finely chop celery, adding to pot as you cut.
   Add spice, curry paste, garlic and ginger. Stir to combine, then **remove from heat**.
   If you want to increase the protein, sauté a chicken breast with the veggies.

   To peel potato and squash quickly, cut in half, place flat side down and remove peel from top to bottom with a knife. Peel skin from potato then cut into small chunks, adding to pot as you cut. Peel squash, remove seeds and cut flesh into small chunks, adding to pot as you cut. Cover with broth and water and bring to a full boil at high heat, then **reduce to simmer**.

   …when oven is preheated…
4. **Turn oven off** and toss bread in.

5. Rinse spinach leaves under cold water in salad spinner and spin dry. Sliver onion finely. Wash and cut orange pepper and cucumber. Divide spinach on serving plates, top with slivered onion, pepper and cucumber slices. Drizzle with salad dressing.

   Reserve 2 cups of soup before serving. Cool and freeze to use with Sicilian Pasta in Week 5.

Ingredients:

Take out ingredients.

1 large sweet potato (1 1/2 to 2 lbs or 675 g to 900 g)
1 butternut squash (2 to 2 1/2 lbs or 900 to 1125 g)

1 tsp butter
1 tsp olive oil, extra-virgin
1 onion
4 celery ribs
1 tsp original, all purpose seasoning, salt-free
1/2 tsp cumin, ground
1/8 tsp salt
1/4 tsp fresh ground pepper
2 tsp curry paste (mild, madras or hot)
   Or more if you are a curry nut!
3 tsp fresh garlic (from a jar)
   (or 3 cloves)
2 tsp ginger (from a jar)
   (or grated fresh)
30 fl oz or 900 mL chicken broth, reduced-sodium
2 cups water

1 multigrain French loaf

6 oz or 170 g prewashed baby spinach
1/8 red onion
1/4 orange bell pepper
1/4 cucumber
1/4 cup salad dressing, light, your favorite

Serves 6

DINNER IS READY IN 30 MINUTES

Equipment List:

Large stove-top pot
Cutting board
Salad spinner
Sharp veggie knife
Bread knife
Can opener
Fine grater
Salad tongs
Soup ladle
Stirring spoon
Fork
Measuring cups and spoons

Per serving:

Calories	377
Fat	8.8 g
Protein	12.9 g
Carbohydrate	63.6 g
Fiber	7.9 g
Sodium	963 mg

15
to
prep

W
E   3
E
K

U.S. Food Exchanges:		Cdn. Food Choices:	
3	Starch	3 1/2	Carb
2	Meat-lean	2	Meat/Alt
1	Fat	1/2	Fat
2	Vegetable	1/2	Other

2 cups of soup set aside for Sicilian Pasta.

Peanut Butter and Honey Chicken, Sweet Potato Fries and Snap Peas

Instructions:

Don't change yet! Take out equipment.

1. Preheat **oven** to 425° F.

2. Soften peanut butter and honey in a small bowl for approx 10 seconds in the **microwave**. Whisk in soy sauce.

   Unravel chicken thighs and flatten on broiler pan. Drizzle peanut butter and honey mixture evenly over chicken, then spread with the back of a spoon. Sprinkle with sesame seeds.

   Place chicken in preheated **oven**. Set timer for 10 minutes.
   Chicken actually cooks for 30-35 minutes or until internal temp is 170° F. Always use an instant read thermometer to ensure the chicken is cooked through, they are only a few bucks and really help you to know when dinner is ready.

   ...when timer rings for chicken, leave chicken in...

3. Spray cookie sheet with sides with cooking spray and heat for 30 seconds in **oven**. Remove pan from oven, scatter fries on pan in a single layer and return to oven. Set timer for 10 minutes. Toss and reset for an additional 10 minutes or follow package directions.

   ...meanwhile...

4. Rinse snap peas in a colander. Add to a large nonstick **fry pan**. Let stand.

   ...when timer rings for chicken and fries...
   Turn heat to high for snap peas. Drizzle with sesame oil and toss until hot and fragrant.
   If you want to skip sautéing them by all means! They are great just as they are!

Ingredients:

Take out ingredients.

2 Tbsp peanut butter, light
2 Tbsp liquid honey
2 tsp soy sauce, reduced-sodium
  (or use Bragg)

10-12 chicken thighs, boneless, skinless (1 3/4 lbs or 800 g)

2 Tbsp sesame seeds

cooking spray

1 lb or 450 g frozen sweet potato fries
  (or regular fries)

1 lb or 450 g snap peas

1/2 tsp sesame oil

Serves 4-6

DINNER IS READY IN 55 MINUTES

Equipment List:

Broiler pan
Large nonstick fry pan
Cookie sheet w/sides
Colander
Small microwave-safe
  mixing bowl
Flipper
Whisk
Stirring spoon
Spoon
Instant read thermometer
Measuring cups and spoons

Per serving:

Calories	393
Fat	14.4 g
Protein	31.0 g
Carbohydrate	34.7 g
Fiber	6.2 g
Sodium	357 mg

U.S. Food Exchanges:		Cdn. Food Choices:	
1	Starch	1	Carb
4	Meat	4	Meat/Alt
1	Vegetable	1/2	Fat
1/2	Other	1	Other

About the Recipes

Blue

Raan is usually done with lamb or goat, but most families wouldn't eat goat and can't afford to purchase a lamb roast, especially in the work week. I got an idea…what if we use beef and convert the leftovers into another meal. So began the beef raan with the leftovers making philly cheese steaks. If you think these spices are too unusual for your family…leave them off and spice your roast the way you normally would….but whatever you do, don't leave out the onion jam!

Green

This is the next best way to have poultry with skin! Yum! I am a health nut, but crave my wings! It's honestly worth purchasing a BBQ cage if only for using it with wings. The fat drips off as you flip and makes them so easy to make. This sauce isn't too hot but has a nice bite!
Vegetarians, toss a veggie based chicken strip sautéed in a little garlic on your Caesar salad.

Blue

I tested many versions of mac and cheese. Most people found them quite plain. Soooo I had an idea…put them side by side with white cheddar mac and cheese from a box. The box won 100% of the time. Soooo just in case you think I'm nuts for using a box of mac and cheese for this…now you know why. The homemade versions are also over the top with fat! So that's my story and now you know I'm not nuts, just trying to make your life easy with better nutritional data!

Red

These are soooo good and fantastic with sautéed strips of portabella for all you vegetarians out there!

Yellow

Every time we travel we try a new version of this! The thing we always hate is lots of times it's too strong with way too much sauce. Soooo I did a stir fry version and the test families just loved it! We do too!
Vegetarians can replace the chicken with veggie strips or just load up on the veggies and add nuts.

Week 4

Blue:

Raan (sort of) with Onion Jam,
Potatoes and Green Beans

Our family rating: 8.5
Your family rating: _____

Green:

Sticky Hot'n Sweet Wings
with Caesar Salad

Our family rating: 10
Your family rating: _____

Blue:

Tuna (or Chicken) Macaroni Bake
with Fresh Veggies

Our family rating: 10
Your family rating: _____

Red:

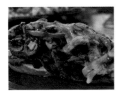

Philly Cheese Steaks
with BLT Salad

Our family rating: 9
Your family rating: _____

Yellow:

Not Your Average General Tso's Chicken
on Vermicelli Pasta

Our family rating: 9
Your family rating: _____

Raan (sort of) with Onion Jam, Potatoes and Green Beans

Instructions:

...the night before...
Take out equipment.
1. Combine the following ingredients in a small bowl to make a paste: cumin, coriander, cardamom, cinnamon, ginger, cloves, pepper, garlic, tomato paste, Sambal Oelek, mustard and balsamic vinegar. Cover roast with paste. Set aside in **fridge**.

...in the morning...
2. Heat **oven** to 425° F. Place roast in oven-safe pan uncovered in preheated **oven**. Set timer for 20 minutes, then reduce heat to 170° F for the rest of the day, up to 9 hours.
...when you arrive home...
3. Remove roast and **reset oven** to 350° F. Wrap roast in foil to rest once internal temp is 140° F in center. *If temp is not 140° F, leave in oven with potatoes until temp is reached.*

4. Wash potatoes and place in a large lasagna or cake pan. Toss with olive oil and spice until potatoes are well coated. Place in preheated **oven**. Set timer for 35 minutes. Potatoes are ready when easily pierced with a knife.

5. Heat oil in a medium nonstick **fry pan** on medium heat. Sliver onion, adding to pan as you cut. **Reduce heat** to medium low and sauté until onion is translucent and very soft. Add water and cook until all water is gone. Add maple syrup and more water and cook until almost all the water is cooked down. **Remove from heat** and set aside at room temp in serving bowl.

...meanwhile...
6. Rinse green beans in colander or steamer basket. Place a small amount of water in the bottom of a **stove-top** pot with beans in the basket above and let stand. When potatoes are ready, bring beans to a full boil. Cover and set timer for 3 minutes...or microwave at high for 3 minutes. Toss with butter if you must.

Ingredients:

Take out ingredients.
Rub for Roast
1 tsp cumin, ground
1 tsp coriander
1 tsp cardamom
1/2 tsp cinnamon, ground
1/2 tsp ginger, ground
1/4 tsp cloves, ground
1/2 tsp fresh ground pepper
1 Tbsp fresh garlic (from a jar)
2 Tbsp tomato paste
1/2 tsp Sambal Oelek (crushed chili paste)
2 tsp sweet hot mustard
1/4 cup balsamic vinegar
5 lbs or 2250 g sirloin roast, boneless, trimmed (or round roast) make sure to use a thick roast
aluminum foil

20 baby potatoes (or 4 potatoes cut into chunks) *If baby potatoes are big, cut in half.*
1 tsp olive oil, extra-virgin
1 tsp original, all purpose seasoning, salt-free

Onion Jam
1 tsp olive oil, extra-virgin
1 onion
1/4 cup water
1 Tbsp maple syrup
1/4 cup water
The onion jam is to eat with your beef. Yum!

1 lb or 450 g frozen whole green beans

butter (optional)

Serves 4-6
Before serving, set aside 3/5 of beef for Philly Cheese Steak later in the week.

DINNER IS READY IN 40 MINUTES

Equipment List:

..the night before...
Small mixing bowl
Stirring spoon
Measuring cups and spoons

...when you arrive home...
Large lasagna or cake-pan
Oven-safe pan
Medium nonstick fry pan
Stove-top pot w/steamer basket
Cutting board
Colander
Serving bowl
Sharp veggie knife
Stirring spoon
Instant read thermometer
Measuring cups and spoons
Aluminum foil

Per serving:

Calories	427
Fat	14.9 g
Protein	36.1 g
Carbohydrate	38.1 g
Fiber	6.0 g
Sodium	114 mg

U.S. Food Exchanges:		Cdn. Food Choices:	
2	Starch	2	Carb
4 1/2	Meat-lean	5	Meat/Alt
1/2	Fat		
1	Vegetable		

3/5 of roast is reserved for Philly Cheese Steak and lunch meal.

Sticky Hot'n Sweet Wings
with Caesar Salad

Instructions:

Don't change yet! Take out equipment.

1. Preheat **BBQ grill** or grill pan to medium (approx 350° F). *You can also use the oven.* Spray a **BBQ grill cage** (or foil grill pan) with cooking spray. *The cage makes grilling easier.* Place wings in cage. Sprinkle with spice. Flip wings every 3-5 minutes or until wings are dark golden brown on all sides and thickest part of largest wing's internal temp is 170° F, approx 20-25 minutes.

   Combine hot sauce and sweet Thai chili sauce in a medium size bowl with lid. *An ice cream bucket works great too.* Set aside.

2. Combine mayonnaise, spice, cheese, lemon juice, garlic, Worcestershire sauce and milk in a medium bowl. Finely chop jalapeños. Add to dressing and stir. Set aside until you are ready to serve.
   You will only use 1/3 cup for the whole salad but it stores well for a couple weeks in the fridge...or use a light prepared Caesar dressing from the store.

   Tear lettuce into bite size pieces directly into salad spinner. Rinse under cold water and spin dry. Place in a large salad bowl.

3. Once wings are cooked, drop them into the bucket of sauce, place the lid on and toss until coated!

4. Drizzle dressing all over lettuce leaves and toss a little at a time until leaves are well coated. You'll know how much you like! Then add Parmesan, croutons and bacon bits. Toss again.

   A little focaccia with oil and vinegar is a nice addition to up your carb content.

Ingredients:

Take out ingredients.

cooking spray
24 split chicken wings
   (approx 3 lbs or 1250 g)
2 tsp garlic and herb seasoning,
   salt-free
<u>Hot'n Sweet Wing Sauce</u>
2 Tbsp hot sauce
3 Tbsp sweet Thai chili sauce
   If you want 'sweeter less hot' wings-increase the sweet Thai sauce and decrease the hot sauce.

<u>Garlic Lovers Caesar Dressing</u>
1 cup mayonnaise, light
1/8 tsp mustard powder
1/8 tsp onion powder
1/4 tsp garlic and herb seasoning, salt-free
2 Tbsp Parmesan cheese, light, grated
2-3 tsp lemon juice
4 cloves garlic (or 2-3 tsp fresh from a jar)
1/4 tsp Worcestershire sauce
2 Tbsp 1% milk, cream or water
4-10 pickled Jalapeño slices (optional for those who love things spicy)

1 head Romaine lettuce

Hot'n Sweet Wing Sauce (previously made)

Garlic Lover's Caesar Dressing
   (previously made)
1 Tbsp Parmesan cheese, light, grated
1/2 cup croutons
1/4 cup real bacon bits (optional)

focaccia bread (optional)
olive oil and balsamic vinegar (optional)

<u>Serves 4-6</u>

DINNER IS READY IN 35 MINUTES

Equipment List:

BBQ grill or grill pan
BBQ grill cage
Medium mixing bowl
Medium mixing bowl w/lid
Cutting board
Salad spinner
Salad bowl
Salad tongs
BBQ tongs
Sharp veggie knife
Mixing spoon
Instant read thermometer
Measuring cups and spoons

Per serving:

Calories	430
Fat	27.5 g
Protein	33.2 g
Carbohydrate	11.7 g
Fiber	2.6 g
Sodium	472 mg

U.S. Food Exchanges:		Cdn. Food Choices:	
1/2	Starch	1	Carb
4	Meat-high fat	5	Meat/Alt
1 1/2	Fat	3	Fat
1/2	Other		

1/3 cup of Caesar Dressing is used.

Tuna (or Chicken) Macaroni Bake with Fresh Veggies

Instructions:

Don't change yet! Take out equipment.

1. Preheat **oven** to 350° F.

2. Fill a large **stove-top** pot with water and bring to a boil for pasta.

   ...meanwhile...

3. Rinse cucumber, pepper and baby carrots. Slice cucumber and sliver pepper. Rinse cauliflower and broccoli and cut into bite size pieces. Arrange on a plate.
   I always place the veggies on the table before dinner. Remember, kids and adults eat more veggies if they eat them first.

4. Place only the macaroni into the boiling water, stir and cook uncovered. Set timer for 2 minutes less than the package directions, approx 6 minutes.

   ...when timer rings for pasta...
   Rinse pasta under hot water in a colander. Let drain and return to pasta pot. Add mushroom soup, milk and cheese packages. Stir to combine.

5. Drain water from tuna and crumble in. Stir. Place macaroni mixture in bottom of an oven-safe casserole dish. Sprinkle or grind fresh pepper on top.

   Top with a layer of cheddar cheese. Bake in preheated **oven**, uncovered. Set timer for 25 minutes.

   If you like your cheese crunchy on top, broil for a few minutes at the end. Watch carefully though—you don't want a big burnt mess!

Ingredients:

Take out ingredients.

water

1/2 English cucumber
1 red bell pepper (or orange bell pepper)
1 cup baby carrots
1 cup cauliflower
1 cup broccoli florets
 (or use 1 package of cut-up
 raw veggies) (1 lb or 450 g)
1/3 cup ranch dressing, fat-free (optional)

2 boxes macaroni and cheese dinner
 (8 oz or 225 g each)
 I like white cheddar.

1 can cream of mushroom soup, reduced-sodium (10 fl oz or 284 mL)
1/2 soup can of 1% milk
cheese packages
 (from mac and cheese boxes)

1 can solid tuna in water, no sodium, drained (6 1/2 oz or 184 g)
 (or use canned or cooked chicken)
1/4 tsp fresh ground pepper

1 cup sharp cheddar cheese, light, shredded

<u>**Serves 4-6**</u>

82

DINNER IS READY IN 40 MINUTES

Equipment List:

Large stove-top pot
Oven-safe casserole dish
Colander
Cutting board
Sharp veggie knife
Serving plate
Can opener
Stirring spoon
Measuring cups and spoons

Per serving:

Calories	433
Fat	8.4 g
Protein	26.7 g
Carbohydrate	62.8 g
Fiber	3.4 g
Sodium	979 mg

U.S. Food Exchanges:		Cdn. Food Choices:	
3	Starch	3	Carb
3	Meat-lean	3 1/2	Meat/Alt
1	Other	1	Other

20 to prep

Philly Cheese Steaks
with BLT Salad

Instructions:

Don't change yet! Take out equipment.

1. Heat oil and butter in a large, wide-bottom, nonstick **fry pan** at medium-low. Sliver onion, adding to pan as you cut. Stir occasionally until soft and caramelized. Rinse and slice mushrooms, adding to pan as you cut. Sliver pepper, adding to pan as you cut. (See page 35 for how to cut peppers). Toss everything for a minute, then transfer to a plate.

2. Slice beef into very thin strips (approx 1 1/2 - 2" long), against the grain, adding to uncleaned pan as you cut. Pour broth over top and season with pepper. Increase temperature to high until broth begins to come to a full boil. **Reduce heat** to a high simmer until almost all the broth has evaporated. **Remove from heat**, stir and let cool.

3. Rinse lettuce in basket of salad spinner and spin dry. Transfer to a salad bowl. Cut tomato into pieces. Add tomato, bacon bits and croutons to bowl. Toss with salad dressing right before serving.

4. Heat oven to **broil**. Slice buns in half lengthwise and place open face on cookie sheet. Evenly distribute meat on bottom halves of each, then top with onion-mushroom-pepper mixture. Place cheese directly on top. Place under broiler until cheese bubbles. *Watch carefully, you may have to remove the top halves while waiting for the cheese to bubble, you don't want them to burn.*

   Once cheese has melted, remove and cover with toasted bun top. Serve alongside salad.

Ingredients:

Take out ingredients.
1 tsp olive oil, extra-virgin
1 tsp butter
1 onion
10 mushrooms
1 green or red bell pepper
If you don't like peppers, leave them out, but it's more authentic with them.

1 1/2 lbs or 675 g very thinly sliced left over roast beef (or thinly sliced deli roast beef)
2 cups beef broth, reduced-sodium
1/4 tsp fresh ground pepper
The Raan spices on the beef already spice the sauce on its own, but I like to add a little extra pepper because we like things a little spicier.

1 head Romaine lettuce
1 tomato
1/4 cup bacon bits
1/2 cup croutons
1/4 - 1/3 cup ranch dressing, fat-free

4 multigrain hot dog buns
 (or 2 sub buns, cut in half)
prepared meat
prepared onion-mushroom-pepper mixture
1/2 cup Italian grated cheese blend
 (or mozzarella cheese, part-skim, shredded)

<u>**Serves 4-6**</u>

DINNER IS READY IN 30 MINUTES

Equipment List:

Large wide-bottom, nonstick
  fry pan
Cookie sheet
2 cutting boards
Sharp veggie knife
Sharp meat knife
Bread knife
Plate
Salad spinner
Salad bowl
Salad tongs
Measuring cups and spoons

Per serving:

Calories	450
Fat	18.8 g
Protein	35.6 g
Carbohydrate	36.4 g
Fiber	5.9 g
Sodium	765 mg

U.S. Food Exchanges:	Cdn. Food Choices:	
1 1/2 Starch	1 1/2	Carb
4 1/2 Meat	5	Meat/Alt
1 Fat	1	Fat
1/2 Other	1/2	Other

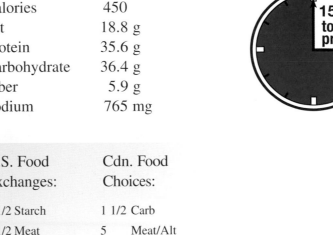

15
to
prep

Not Your Average General Tso's Chicken on Vermicelli Pasta

Instructions:

Don't change yet! Take out equipment.
1. Fill a large **stove-top** pot with water and bring to a boil for pasta.

2. Heat oil in a large nonstick **fry pan** or wok at medium-high. Cut chicken into bite size pieces, adding to pan as you cut. Toss until nicely browned. Add garlic and ginger.

   Rinse and slice mushrooms, adding to pan as you cut. Wash and cut broccoli into small florets, adding to pan as you cut. Rinse and cut green beans in half, adding to pan as you cut. Toss to sauté. **Reduce heat** to medium.

   …meanwhile…
   Combine cornstarch and sugar in a small 2 cup bowl, in that order. Stir to blend. Gradually add water, whisking so that it doesn't lump. Add hoisin, vinegar and soy sauce. Stir to blend. Pour over chicken.

3. Place pasta in boiling water and set timer according to package directions, approximately 5 minutes.

   …when timer rings for pasta…
   Rinse pasta in colander and let drain. Return pasta to pot, cover, **no heat**.

4. To serve, place pasta in the bottom of a bowl. Place veggies and chicken on top of the pasta using a slotted spoon. With a different spoon or ladle, drizzle with sauce.
   A little sauce goes a long way. You don't want to drown the noodles or it tastes too strong. Start with a little, then add if needed.

   We love to sprinkle hot chili flakes and crushed peanuts on top!

Ingredients:

Take out ingredients.
water

1 tsp sesame oil
3 chicken breasts, boneless, skinless (1 lb or 450 g)
1 tsp fresh garlic (from a jar) (or 1 clove minced)
1 tsp ginger, grated (from a jar)
15 button mushrooms (or 8 mushrooms quartered)
1/2 lb or 225 g broccoli florets
1 cup green beans (fresh or frozen, rinsed or 1 small zucchini) *We also like to sliver a little red pepper if we have it on hand.*

1 Tbsp cornstarch
2 tsp brown sugar
1 cup water
1/3 cup hoisin sauce
2 Tbsp rice vinegar
1 Tbsp soy sauce, reduced-sodium

12 oz or 340 g vermicelli pasta (use regular vermicelli or spaghettini, only use rice vermicelli if there are wheat allegeries in your family)

hot chili flakes (optional)
peanuts, crushed (optional)

<u>Serves 4-6</u>

DINNER IS READY IN 25 MINUTES

Equipment List:

Large stove-top pot w/lid
Large nonstick fry pan
Colander
2 cutting boards
Sharp meat knife
Sharp veggie knife
Small mixing bowl
Slotted spoon
Serving spoon
Whisk
Measuring cups and spoons

Per serving:

Calories	358
Fat	2.6 g
Protein	24.9 g
Carbohydrate	60.2 g
Fiber	2.2 g
Sodium	395 mg

U.S. Food Exchanges:		Cdn. Food Choices:	
4	Starch	4	Carb
3	Meat- very lean	3	Meat/Alt

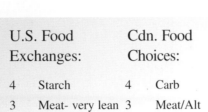

About the Recipes

Yellow

I don't know what it is with me and tortellini in soup, but it's just one of those things that turns soup into a filling, stick to the ribs meal for me! You can add more spice or hot sauce for a spicier version.

Vegetarians, you can leave out the chicken and add mixed beans or pressed tofu. The reason I always put my pasta in the bottom of the bowl instead of right into the soup is so it doesn't get mushy, especially by the next day!

Blue

These empanadas are sooo good. One of the test families mentioned they made smaller ones as the meat didn't fit. Divide the meat into four and stretch the pastry over top to make it fit. Be fearless! Also, I recommend using the sheets vs the blocks of puff pastry. The sheets come in the same size box as phyllo pastry. This makes it even easier 'cause you don't need to roll pastry out!

Vegetarians, veggie grind works beautifully!

Green

Chili chicken—yum yum yum! There is nothing left to say other than that! Okay, just one thing—one test family found this dry even though they loved the flavor. I recommend you set the timer for less time the first time you make it, then check its doneness, juuuust in case your oven's temp is off and cooks hot! This is one of my favorite thigh recipes!

Yellow

The flavor of this pasta is similar to one I ate at an Italian restaurant. You start eating it and think…nice! Then you eat more and keep wanting more!

I love that you can use the leftover squash soup to make it and I love that you can easily convert it to a vegetarian dish by leaving out the sausage.

Red

I'm always trying to come up with new pizza ideas because I know how easy pizza is to make (or double up so you have lunches the next day)! I also love the fact parents can make a simpler kind of pizza, in addition to their bistro variety, without making two separate meals. Our test families loved this.

Vegetarians, use veggie based chicken strips.

Week 5

Yellow: Chicken Tortellini Soup

Our family rating: 10
Your family rating: _____

Blue: Beef Empanadas with Papaya
& Toasted Pumpkin Seed Salad

Our family rating: 9.5
Your family rating: _____

Green: Chili-Glazed Chicken with Rice and Broccoli

Our family rating: 9.5
Your family rating: _____

Yellow: Sicilian Penne Pasta

Our family rating: 9.5
Your family rating: _____

Red: BBQ Southwest Pizza

Our family rating: 8
Your family rating: _____

Chicken Tortellini Soup

Instructions:

Don't change yet! Take out equipment.

1. Fill a large **stove-top** pot with water and bring to a boil for pasta.

2. Heat olive oil in a different large **stove-top** pot at medium. Sliver onion, adding to pot as you cut. Cut celery and carrots into chunks, adding to pot as you cut.
   Cut chicken into bite size pieces, adding to pot as you cut.

   Add broth, water, spice, Worcestershire sauce and hot sauce to pot.

   I usually use a salad kit with this, but if I don't even have time for that I toss in some frozen mixed veggies.

3. Place pasta in boiling water and set timer according to package directions, approx 8 minutes.

   ...when timer rings for pasta...
   Rinse pasta in colander and let drain.

4. To serve, place tortellini in the bottom of your bowl and ladle hot soup over top.

Ingredients:

Take out ingredients.
water

1 tsp olive oil, extra-virgin
1 onion
2 celery ribs
2 carrots
2 cups cooked roaster chicken (from a deli) or use leftover chicken or pork or sauté cut up chicken breast
3 1/2 - 4 cups chicken broth, reduced-sodium
2 1/2 cups water
1/4 tsp celery salt
1/4 tsp poultry seasoning
1/4 tsp fresh ground pepper
1 tsp garlic and herb seasoning, salt-free
1 tsp Worcestershire sauce
1 tsp hot sauce (optional)
1 cup frozen mixed veggies (optional)
salad kit (optional)

4 cups cheese tortellini
   (found in deli section)

Serves 6

DINNER IS READY IN 30 MINUTES

Equipment List:

- 2 large stove-top pots
- 2 cutting boards
- Colander
- Ladle
- Sharp veggie knife
- Sharp meat knife
- Measuring cups and spoons

Per serving:

Calories	341
Fat	9.3 g
Protein	24.1 g
Carbohydrate	40.3 g
Fiber	2.7 g
Sodium	737 mg

U.S. Food Exchanges:	Cdn. Food Choices:
2 1/2 Starch	2 1/2 Carb
3 Meat	3 Meat/Alt
1 Vegetable	

20 to prep

WEEK 5

Beef Empanadas
with Papaya & Toasted Pumpkin Seed Salad

Instructions:

Don't change yet! Take out equipment.
1. Preheat **oven** to 375° F.

2. Heat oil in a large nonstick **fry pan** or wok at med-high. Sliver onion, adding to pan as you cut. Stir occasionally until soft and translucent. Add beef, spices and garlic, stirring until beef is no longer pink.

   Add wine and simmer until no liquid remains. Add salsa, cilantro and fresh pepper, stirring until combined. Set timer for 5 minutes stirring occasionally, then **remove from heat**.

3. Cut puff pastry sheet into 4 equal parts. Prepare one square at a time by brushing water onto two edges of square. Place meat mixture into center of square. Bring opposite tips together to form a triangle over meat. Tuck each tip under and seal edge by crimping with a fork (as shown). Place on cookie sheet. Repeat. *If you brush the tops with a little milk it will help them brown.* Bake in preheated **oven**. Set timer for 20 minutes or until golden brown.

   …while empanadas are cooking…
4. Heat dry **fry pan** at medium-high heat. Add pumpkin seeds to pan and toss until they begin to pop and turn brown. **Remove from heat** and let cool.
   Rinse greens in basket of salad spinner and spin dry. Place on individual plates. Wash and slice papaya, red pepper and sliver red onion, arranging on greens as you slice.

   Whisk together maple syrup, vinegar and dry mustard (you can also add the papaya seeds in for a peppery taste or strain them out when serving). Sprinkle pumpkin seeds over salad.

   We like the empanadas with sides of salsa and sour cream.

Ingredients:

Take out ingredients.

1 tsp olive oil, extra-virgin
1 onion
1 lb or 450 g ground beef, extra-lean
1/8 tsp cinnamon, ground
1/8 tsp cloves, ground
1/2 tsp cumin, ground
1 tsp chili powder
3 tsp fresh garlic (from a jar)
1/4 cup Dubonnet (sweet red wine found in liquor store or sweet sherry)
1 cup chunky salsa (mild, medium or hot)
1/4 cup cilantro, chopped
fresh ground pepper (to your liking)

1 sheet frozen puff pastry (8 oz or 225 g)
If purchasing in blocks, cut one block into 4. Dust flat surface with flour and roll out each square to approx 4"x 4" with a rolling pin or wine bottle.
water

milk (optional)

3 Tbsp raw pumpkin seeds

1 bag mixed salad greens (6 oz or 170 g)
1/4 small papaya (or melon)
1/4 red bell pepper
1/8 red onion

Papaya Salad Dressing (or bottled)
2 Tbsp maple syrup
3 Tbsp white wine vinegar
1/2 tsp dry mustard
2 tsp papaya seeds (optional)

1/2 cup salsa (optional)
1/2 cup sour cream, light (optional)
Serves 4-6

DINNER IS READY IN 40 MINUTES

Equipment List:

2 large nonstick fry pans
Cutting board
Colander
Cookie sheet
Salad spinner
Sharp veggie knife
Stirring spoon
Whisk
Rolling pin
  if using block pastry
Measuring cups and spoons

Per serving:

Calories	409
Fat	22.9 g
Protein	20.4 g
Carbohydrate	30.6 g
Fiber	3.6 g
Sodium	572 mg

U.S. Food Exchanges:		Cdn. Food Choices:	
1 1/2	Starch	1 1/2	Carb
3	Meat	3	Meat
3	Fat	3	Fat
1/2	Other	1/2	Other

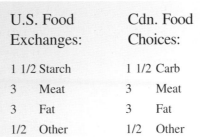

20 to prep

Chili-Glazed Chicken with Rice and Broccoli

Instructions:

Don't change yet! Take out equipment.
1. Preheat **oven** to 350° F.

2. Combine rice and water in an oven-safe pot with lid. Stir, cover and place in **oven** (even if it hasn't preheated yet).

3. Stir chili powder, cumin, balsamic vinegar, honey and chicken broth together in the bottom of a 9"x13" oven-safe baking dish or pan using a fork.

    Unravel thighs, then flatten and scrunch together, smooth side down, on top of combined ingredients in oven-safe baking dish or pan. Once coated, flip so smooth side is up. Place in **preheated oven** beside rice. Set timer for 40 minutes or until internal temperature is 170° F. *Always use an instant read thermometer to ensure the chicken is cooked through, they are only a few bucks and really help you to know when dinner is ready.*

4. Rinse broccoli in colander or steamer basket. Place a small amount of water in the bottom of a **stove-top** pot and place broccoli in the basket above. Let stand.

    ...when timer rings for chicken and rice...
    Bring broccoli water to a full boil. Cover and set timer for 3 minutes...or microwave at high for 3 minutes.
    Toss with butter if you must.

    While the broccoli is cooking, I like to take the thighs and turn them to coat the tops in the sauce again. Flip them back to smooth side up when serving on the plate, they look juicier that way. The sauce is amaaaazing on the rice!!!

Ingredients:

Take out ingredients.

1 1/2 cups basmati rice
(or mixed rice as shown) *I like Canoe brand.*
3 cups of water

1 tsp chili powder
1/2 tsp cumin, ground
2 Tbsp balsamic vinegar
2 Tbsp honey (liquid or softened)
1/4 cup chicken broth, reduced-sodium

10-12 chicken thighs, boneless, skinless
(1 3/4 lbs or 800 g) (or 4-6 chicken breasts)

1 lb or 450 g broccoli florets
water

butter (optional)

Serves 4-6

DINNER IS READY IN 45 MINUTES

Equipment List:

Oven-safe pot w/lid
9"x13" oven-safe baking dish
Stove-top pot w/steamer basket
Colander
Cutting board
Flipper
Fork
Sharp veggie knife
Instant read thermometer
Measuring cups and spoons

Per serving:

Calories	362
Fat	6.0 g
Protein	31.4 g
Carbohydrate	45.2 g
Fiber	1.2 g
Sodium	161 mg

U.S. Food Exchanges:		Cdn. Food Choices:	
2 1/2	Starch	3	Carb
4	Meat-lean	4	Meat/Alt

15
to
prep

W
E
E
K
5

Sicilian Penne Pasta

Instructions:

Don't change yet! Take out equipment.

1. Heat a large nonstick **electric** or **stove-top fry pan** at medium. Break sausage meat into small chunks with your fingers, adding to pan as you break. Cook until meat is no longer pink. *Once the sausage is browned, I like to toss the chunks onto a paper towel, on a plate, to remove excess oil. I then use the paper towel to wipe the pan before putting them back in.* Finely chop onion, adding to pan as you cut. Slice mushrooms, bell peppers and zucchini, in that order, adding to pan as you cut. Add spice.

2. Fill a large **stove-top** pot with water and bring to a boil for pasta.

    ...meanwhile...

3. Add soup, salsa and water to sausage and veggie pan, stirring to combine. Let simmer at medium-low. Stir from time to time.

4. When water comes to a boil, add pasta. Set timer according to package directions, approx 11 minutes.

    ...when timer rings for pasta...
    Rinse pasta in a colander and return to pot, **no heat**. Toss with a little basil and olive oil if you like.

    We serve this as a meal in one with a little pasta in the bottom of a wide bowl smothered in sauce. We also love a sprinkle of Parmesan on top...and hot chili flakes for those who like things spicier!

Ingredients:

Take out ingredients.
1 lb or 450 g Italian sausage meat (hot or mild)
You can take 4 Tbsp out of the sausage meat for the Italian Sausage Stuffed Chicken in Week 9. It won't make a difference in this recipe and then you won't have to buy 2 packages.
paper towel (optional)
1 onion
10 mushrooms
1/2 green bell pepper
1/2 red bell pepper
1 small to medium zucchini
1/2 tsp Italian seasoning
1/2 tsp oregano

water

16 fl oz or 500 mL curried squash, carrot or pumpkin soup (reserved from Curried Butternut Squash Soup, pg 72 or purchased)
1 cup salsa (mild, medium or hot)
1 cup water

3 cups penne pasta
You might want to make extra pasta for leftovers.

1/2 tsp dried basil (optional)
1/2 tsp olive oil, extra-virgin (optional)

Parmesan cheese, light, grated (optional)
hot chili flakes (optional)

<u>Serves 4-6</u>

DINNER IS READY IN 25 MINUTES

Equipment List:

Large stove-top pot
Large nonstick electric
  or stove-top fry pan
Cutting board
Colander
Can opener
Fine grater
Sharp veggie knife
Plate
Serving spoon
Stirring spoon
Measuring cups and spoons
Paper towel

Per serving:

Calories	535
Fat	25.9 g
Protein	21.3 g
Carbohydrate	54.5 g
Fiber	4.9 g
Sodium	892 mg

U.S. Food Exchanges:		Cdn. Food Choices:	
3	Starch	3	Carb
2	Meat-high fat	3	Meat/Alt
2	Fat	3	Fat
1	Vegetable	1/2	Other

20
to
prep

BBQ Southwest Pizza

Instructions:

Don't change yet! Take out equipment.

1. Preheat **oven** to 375º F.

2. Heat oil in a large nonstick **fry pan** at medium-high. Cut meat into bite size pieces, adding to pan as you cut. Add spice and garlic while meat is browning. When meat is no longer pink, set aside on plate.

3. Sliver onion, adding to uncleaned pan as you sliver. Sliver peppers, adding to pan as you cut. Add salsa, Worcestershire sauce and vinegar to pan. Stir to combine and simmer until thick. **Remove from heat**.

4. Brush pizza base with olive oil. Layer in this order: pepper mixture, cooked chicken, then cover with cheese. Place in preheated **oven**. Set timer for 8 minutes or until cheese has melted.

   …while pizza is baking…
5. Wash and cut cold veggies. Arrange on serving plate or display in the colander, as shown.

6. **...when timer rings for pizza...**
   Drizzle with BBQ sauce and sour cream. Sliver lettuce and sprinkle on top as a garnish.

   If I have the time, I also cut up tomato and green onion and sprinkle that on top too!

Ingredients:

Take out ingredients.

1 tsp canola oil
2 chicken breasts, boneless, skinless (3/4 lb or 340 g)
1 tsp cumin, ground
1 tsp chili powder
1 tsp fresh garlic (from a jar)

1 onion
1/2 green bell pepper
1/2 red bell pepper
1/2 cup chunky salsa (mild, medium or hot)
1 Tbsp Worcestershire sauce
1 Tbsp balsamic vinegar

12" thin crust pizza base (1/2 lb or 225 g)
2 tsp olive oil, extra-virgin
prepared pepper mixture
precooked chicken
1 cup mozzarella cheese, part-skim, shredded

3 celery ribs
2 cups baby carrots
1/4 head cauliflower
1 red bell pepper
ranch dressing, fat-free, for dip (optional)

1 Tbsp Southwest BBQ sauce
2 Tbsp sour cream, light
2 Romaine lettuce leaves
   (or sliver green leaves from mixed greens)
tomato (optional)
green onion (optional)

<u>Serves 4</u>

DINNER IS READY IN 25 MINUTES

Equipment List:

Large nonstick fry pan
Colander
2 cutting boards
Sharp veggie knife
Sharp meat knife
Stirring spoon
Cheese grater
Pastry brush
Spoon
Plate
Measuring cups and spoons

Per serving:

Calories	482
Fat	14.4 g
Protein	37.3 g
Carbohydrate	53.7 g
Fiber	9.0 g
Sodium	928 mg

U.S. Food Exchanges:		Cdn. Food Choices:	
2	Starch	2	Carb
4 1/2	Meat	5	Meat/Alt
1	Other	1	Other

15
to
prep

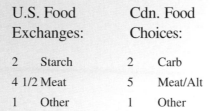

About the Recipes

Red

I loooove going out for Vietnamese food! One of my all time favorite things to order is Lemongrass Chicken. I finally sat down one day and thought…I'm sure I can figure out how to make this quick but keep it tasting just like the one I eat out! So on went the creative challenge—I was so thrilled when I nailed it!

Vegetarians, use thin strips of veggie based chicken.

Red

This is so fresh tasting! It's really cool to add just that one rib of fennel. It adds this little unexpected taste! When you steal it from the root you are using for the bacon, fennel and tomato pasta sauce this week, you'll really get it how fennel can taste so wonderful and so different in separate dishes!

Vegetarians who don't eat fish will find this lovely by following the first step then adding the raisins and mandarin. Put that in a portabella mushroom with cheese and nuts on top…Heeeelllo!

Blue

I know tamale pie has a corn meal crust, but this is a way to avoid making pastry while getting the same sort of flavor! When you follow the directions on page 33 for draping the pastry, you'll see why this is the perfect entertaining dish because it looks amazing no matter what you do…you can't screw it up!

Veggie grind works great in this!

Yellow

I remember the first time I tried something similar to this. I couldn't get over how the flavors of fennel and tomato played on each other! This is sooooo simple to make, but remember it's very low calorie and low on protein, so if that's a concern for you I really recommend upping the protein with either chicken breast or its veggie counterpart!

Vegetarians…hold the bacon!

Green

This is such a wonderful entertaining dish! It always looks great and the pork is always beautiful! The flavor is out of this world!

Vegetarians…poke baker's potatoes with a fork and microwave until the potato can be easily pierced with a knife. Let cool, cut in half and hollow out. Then combine the potato with cheese and broccoli, put the mixture back on top of potato skin with pesto and panko and broil! Really nice! Serve with edamame beans in the shell sautéed with soy sauce and lemon pepper!

Week 6

Red: Lemongrass Chicken
on Rice with Broccoli

Our family rating: 10
Your family rating: _____

Red: Salmon with Mandarins, Mixed Rice
and Asparagus

Our family rating: 8.5
Your family rating: _____

Blue: Tamale Pie (sort of) with Fruit Salad
Our family rating: 9
Your family rating: _____

Yellow: Bacon, Fennel & Tomato Penne Pasta
with Green Beans
Our family rating: 10
Your family rating: _____

Green: Pesto-Dijon Pork Chops
with Roasted Potatoes and Peas

Our family rating: 9.5
Your family rating: _____

Lemongrass Chicken on Rice with Broccoli

Instructions:

...the night before...

Take out equipment.

1. Combine fish sauce, garlic, curry powder and sugar in a large mixing bowl.
   Cut chicken into strips, against the grain, adding to bowl as you cut. Toss to coat, cover and place in **fridge**.

...when you arrive home...

2. Combine rice and water in a large microwave-safe pot with lid. **Microwave** at high for 8 minutes, then medium for 8 minutes. Place a paper towel under the pot for spills.

3. Rinse broccoli in colander or steamer basket. Place a small amount of water in the bottom of a **stove-top** pot and bring to a full boil with the broccoli in the basket above. Cover and set timer for 3 minutes...or microwave at high for 3 minutes. When timer rings, **remove from heat** and let stand.

...meanwhile...

4. Heat oil in a nonstick **fry pan** at med-low. Finely chop shallot, adding to pan as you cut. Trim lemongrass on both ends so you are left with the bulb. Pound with a mallet or kitchen hammer, then finely chop (see page 35). Discard the stringy, long parts. Add the rest to pan.

   Cut chilies in half and remove seeds. *Wash your hands and don't rub your eyes.* Finely chop chilies, adding to pan as you cut. **Increase heat** to high. Add bowl of marinated chicken. Toss until no longer pink.

   Sprinkle with sugar, toss again, then add water. Once chicken has a light glaze, serve immediately over rice.

   We like to garnish with slivered green onion and crushed peanuts. This recipe tastes just like the restaurant version with less fat, sugar and salt aaaaand with a lot fewer steps!

Ingredients:

Take out ingredients.

2 Tbsp fish sauce
2 tsp fresh garlic (from a jar)
1 Tbsp curry powder
1 1/2 tsp sugar
1 1/2 lbs or 675 g chicken thighs, boneless, skinless

1 1/2 cups basmati rice
3 cups water
paper towel

1 lb or 450 g broccoli florets
water

1 Tbsp canola or peanut oil
1-2 shallots
2 stalks lemongrass

2-3 red Thai chilies
prepared strips of chicken

2 Tbsp sugar
1/4 cup water

green onion, for garnish (optional)
peanuts (optional)

<u>Serves 4-6</u>

DINNER IS READY IN 30 MINUTES

Equipment List:

...the night before...
Large mixing bowl
Cutting board
Sharp meat knife
Stirring spoon
Measuring spoons

...when you arrive home...
Large nonstick fry pan
Large microwave-safe pot w/lid
Stove-top pot w/steamer basket
Colander
Cutting board
Sharp veggie knife
Mallet
Measuring cups and spoons
Paper towel

Per serving:

Calories	377
Fat	7.8 g
Protein	28.3 g
Carbohydrate	48.4 g
Fiber	1.7 g
Sodium	586 mg

U.S. Food Exchanges:	Cdn. Food Choices:
2 1/2 Starch	2 1/2 Carb
3 Meat	4 Meat/Alt
1/2 Other	1/2 Other

15
to
prep

W
E
E
K

6

Salmon with Mandarins, Mixed Rice and Asparagus

Instructions:

Don't change yet! Take out equipment.

1. Heat oil and butter in a large nonstick **fry pan** at medium heat.
   Finely chop onion, adding to pan as you cut. Sauté until caramelized. Finely chop fennel and add to pan. Sauté until tender but still a little firm, approx 5 minutes.
   Transfer onion and fennel to a small bowl. Do not wash pan.

2. Combine rice and water in a large microwave safe pot with lid. **Microwave** at high for 8 minutes, then medium for 8 minutes. Place a paper towel under the pot in case of spills.

3. Snap off bottom nodes of asparagus and discard. Rinse in colander or steamer basket. Place a small amount of water in the bottom of a **stove-top** pot. Let stand.

4. Spray uncleaned onion pan with cooking spray. Rinse salmon under cold water, pat dry with a paper towel and season one side. Sauté, spice side down, over medium heat, approx 3 minutes. Season, flip and sauté other side. Add onion, fennel, raisins and mandarin to pan. Cover and let steam for 3-5 minutes or until internal temperature of salmon is 155° F.

5. Bring asparagus water to a full boil with the asparagus in the basket above. Cover and set timer for 4 minutes...or microwave for the same amount of time. When timer rings, **remove from heat**. Drain water and toss in pot with a little butter if you must.

This is so simple yet so delicious!

Ingredients:

Take out ingredients.
1 tsp olive oil, extra-virgin
1 tsp butter
1/4 red onion
1 rib base fennel root
<u>NOTE:</u> The remainder is for **Bacon, Fennel & Tomato Penne Pasta** this week. See page 108.

1 1/2 cups mixed rice (white and wild)
I like Canoe brand.
3 cups water
paper towel

20 asparagus spears (1 lb or 450 g)

cooking spray
4-6 salmon filets, boneless, skinless, (1 1/2 lbs or 675 g) (or butterfly chicken so it cooks at the same rate)
paper towel
1/2 tsp oregano leaves
2 tsp garlic and herb seasoning, salt-free
prepared onion-fennel mix
1 Tbsp raisins
1 Mandarin orange

butter (optional)

<u>Serves 4-6</u>

DINNER IS READY IN 25 MINUTES

Equipment List:

Large nonstick fry pan w/lid
Large microwave-safe pot w/lid
Stove-top pot w/steamer basket
Small mixing bowl
Colander
Flipper
Cutting board
Sharp veggie knife
Stirring spoon
Measuring cups and spoons
Paper towel

Per serving:

Calories	335
Fat	6.2 g
Protein	28.2 g
Carbohydrate	41.6 g
Fiber	2.7 g
Sodium	108 mg

U.S. Food Exchanges:	Cdn. Food Choices:
2 1/2 Starch	2 1/2 Carb
3 Meat-lean	4 Meat/Alt
1/2 Fruit	

15 to prep

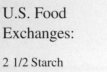

W
E
E
K

6

Tamale Pie (sort of) with Fruit Salad

Instructions:

Don't change yet! Take out equipment.
1. Preheat **oven** to 375° F.

2. Heat oil in a large nonstick **fry pan** at medium-low. Sliver onion, adding to pan as you cut. Stir occasionally until soft and caramelized.
Add beef and spices to fry pan. Break up the beef with a spoon. Brown until no longer pink.

Coarsely chop green pepper, adding to pan as you cut. Add corn, salsa, cheese and chili flakes. **Reduce heat** to simmer for 10 minutes.

…meanwhile…
(see page 33 for illustrations)
3. Pinch 2 triangles together to form a rectangle. Stretch lengthwise to drape over half of the inside and outside wall of an 8" or 9" springform pan. Repeat over other side of pan. Press firmly to completely cover inside wall. *There is no pastry on the bottom of the pan.* Pour the meat mixture into the pan. Bring the outside pastry to the center on top of mixture. If it looks like it doesn't quite fit – you've done it right! Pinch together what you can leaving a few vent holes.
Place in preheated **oven**. Set timer for 25 minutes or until top is dark golden brown.

…meanwhile…
4. Wash and cut melon into bite size pieces. Rinse blackberries, strawberries and grapes.

…when timer rings for pie…
Serve alongside fruit salad. *We love a little vanilla yogurt on our fruit.*
Some of my kids love sour cream or salsa with the pie. I also like hot chili flakes, yum!

Ingredients:

Take out ingredients.

1 tsp olive oil, extra-virgin
1 onion
1 1/2 lbs or 675 g ground beef, extra-lean
1 Tbsp chili powder
1 tsp Italian seasoning
fresh ground pepper to taste

1/2 green bell pepper
1 cup frozen corn, rinsed
1 1/2 cups salsa (mild, medium or hot)
1 cup cheddar cheese, light, shredded
1 tsp hot chili flakes (optional)
If you know everyone likes spicier food, add to ground beef mix.

1 pkg Pillsbury Crescent Rolls
(8 oz or 225 g)

prepared meat mixture

2 cups cantaloupe or honey dew melon
3/4 cup blackberries (or other berries)
1 cup strawberries
1 cup green seedless grapes

vanilla yogurt, low-fat (optional)

sour cream, light (optional)
salsa (mild, medium or hot) (optional)
hot chili flakes (optional)

<u>Serves 6</u>

DINNER IS READY IN 50 MINUTES

Equipment List:

Large nonstick fry pan
8" or 9" springform pan
Cutting board
Colander
Sharp veggie knife
Stirring spoon
Cheese grater
Measuring cups and spoons

Per serving:

Calories	508
Fat	24.8 g
Protein	31.1 g
Carbohydrate	40.8 g
Fiber	4.8 g
Sodium	886 mg

U.S. Food Exchanges:		Cdn. Food Choices:	
1 1/2	Starch	2 1/2	Carb
4	Meat-lean	4	Meat/Alt
3	Fat	3	Fat
1	Fruit		

20 to prep

WEEK 6

Bacon, Fennel & Tomato Penne Pasta with Green Beans

Instructions:

Don't change yet! Take out equipment.

1. Trim the root end and rib ends from the fennel root (you only use the root). See page 33 for illustrations. *Save a little of the feathery herb looking part for garnish on top of pasta.* Slice root in half then cut into 1/4" thick slivers. Rinse thoroughly under water in a colander.

   Heat oil and butter in a large nonstick **fry pan** at medium heat. Add fennel to pan. Coarsely chop garlic, adding to pan as you cut. Cut bacon into 1/2" pieces, adding to pan as you cut. Cook until fennel is just soft.

   Add tomatoes with liquid and spice. **Reduce heat** to a low simmer and cook uncovered, stirring occasionally.

   …meanwhile…

2. Fill a large **stove-top** pot with water, cover and bring to a boil. Place pasta in boiling water, stir and cook uncovered. Set timer according to package directions, approx 11 minutes.

3. Rinse beans in colander or steamer basket. Place a small amount of water in the bottom of a **stove-top** pot and bring to a full boil with the beans in the basket above. Cover and set timer for 3 minutes...or microwave at high for 3 minutes. When timer rings, **remove from heat** and let stand.

4. Crush croutons. Set aside.
   ...when timer rings for pasta...
   Drain pasta and rinse under hot water in colander. Return to pasta pot and toss in a small amount of olive oil if you wish.

   On each plate, place noodles, sauce and sprinkle with crushed croutons. *A sprinkle of Parmesan and a few feathery fennel sprigs looks and tastes great too!*

Ingredients:

Take out ingredients.
1 fennel root bulb (sometimes called anise)
NOTE: Save one rib base for **Salmon with Mandarins** this week. See page 104.

1 tsp olive oil, extra-virgin
1 tsp butter
5 cloves garlic (or 3-4 tsp fresh garlic from a jar)
7 strips fully cooked bacon, low-sodium purchase this way (for more protein you can also add sautéed chicken breast)
1 can Italian stewed tomatoes (28 fl oz or 796 mL)
1/4 tsp fresh ground pepper
1/2 tsp hot chili flakes (use less if you don't like it spicy)

water

3 1/2 cups penne pasta

1 lb or 450 g frozen green beans

8 croutons (optional)

1/2 tsp olive oil, extra-virgin (optional)

Parmesan cheese, light, grated (optional)

Serves 4-6

DINNER IS READY IN 30 MINUTES

Equipment List:

Large nonstick fry pan
Large stove-top pot
Stove-top pot w/steamer basket
Colander
Cutting board
Sharp veggie knife
Can opener
Measuring cups and spoons

Per serving:

Calories	365
Fat	5.0 g
Protein	14.2 g
Carbohydrate	67.9 g
Fiber	7.2 g
Sodium	473 mg

U.S. Food Exchanges:		Cdn. Food Choices:	
3 1/2	Starch	4	Carb
1	Meat	2	Meat/Alt
1/2	Fat		
1	Vegetable		

20 to prep

W
E
E
K 6

Pesto-Dijon Pork Chops
with Roasted Potatoes and Peas

Instructions:

Don't change yet! Take out equipment.

1. Preheat **oven** to 450° F.

2. Place potatoes in a metal lasagna or cake pan. If the baby potatoes are large, cut them in half. Drizzle with olive oil and sprinkle with spice. Toss to completely coat, then place in **oven** (don't wait for the oven to preheat).

3. Rinse peas in colander or steamer basket. Place a small amount of water in the bottom of a **stove-top** pot. Let stand.

4. Combine pesto and Dijon in a small bowl or cup.
   Place pork chops on a broiler pan. Spread pesto-Dijon mixture evenly over each pork chop. Sprinkle with panko flakes.

   Once temperature reaches 450° F, **reduce heat** to 425° F. Place pork chops in **oven** beside potatoes. Set timer for 20 minutes.

   ...when timer rings...

5. Bring water to a full boil with the peas in the basket above. Cover and set timer for 2-3 minutes...or microwave at high for 3-4 minutes.

   ...meanwhile...

6. Remove potatoes from oven when pierced easily with a knife.

7. **Broil** pork chops until tops are just brown. *Watch carefully, you don't want a burnt mess!*

Ingredients:

Take out ingredients.

20 baby potatoes (or 4 large, thin skin, cut into smaller chunks)
1 tsp olive oil, extra-virgin
1/2 tsp original, all purpose seasoning, salt-free

3 cups frozen baby peas

1/4 cup basil pesto (found near pasta sauces)
1 Tbsp Dijon mustard
4 large pork loin chops, 1/2" thick, boneless, trimmed (1 1/2 lbs or 675 g)
1/4 cup panko flakes (found near coating mixes) *Bug your local grocery store to carry these if they don't have them. These are great to have on hand!*

Serves 4-6

DINNER IS READY IN 40 MINUTES

Equipment List:

Broiler pan
Stove-top pot w/steamer basket
Metal lasagna or cake pan
Colander
Small bowl or cup
Stirring spoon
Measuring cups and spoons

Per serving:

Calories	381
Fat	8.7 g
Protein	34.5 g
Carbohydrate	40.9 g
Fiber	6.7 g
Sodium	405 mg

U.S. Food Exchanges:		Cdn. Food Choices:	
2	Starch	2 1/2	Carb
4 1/2	Meat-lean	5	Meat/Alt
1	Vegetable		

15
to
prep

W
E
E
K

6

About the Recipes

Green

It's yummy ham! Ham is a great weekday meal because it gives you leftovers for amazing lunches! Also, if ham isn't something you buy often make sure you get one a little bigger so you can freeze 2 cups cubed for the Ham Strata in week 10.
This hot sweet mustard is soooo amazing on ham sandwiches.

Yellow

YUM YUM YUM! This great, quick pasta dish was a favorite with the test families and easy to make with pressed tofu for a vegetarian option! I got these dishes at Pottery Barn. They are so fun to serve dinner in and you can pop them right into the dishwasher!

Yellow

Get ready for entertaining! The authentic version is served with a rim of mashed potato then baked. It's yummy, but more finicky! I decided to try it in the puff pastry patty shells instead and they are a hit! These are also easy as you are able to make the shells ahead of time!
If you are vegetarian, but do not eat seafood, make it with cut up veggie chicken.

Blue

Ok folks—Dubonnet is going to be your best cooking friend this year! It's often less than $10 a bottle and you can use it any time a recipe says marsala wine or sweet sherry. The alcohol burns off so you don't have to worry about the kids! Think of it as a specialty condiment that you can use over and over…see page 26.
Vegetarians…do everything the same using a portabella. Cut up broccoli to sauté with the onion instead of using mushrooms. Keep the components separate then top with the onion-broccoli mixture and pour the sauce over top! You will need to up your protein though!

Red

One of my new favorite soups! So hearty, so fun and sooo delicious! This slow cooker meal can be left on low heat for up to 10 hours.
Vegetarians…we had to sauté the veggie grind so you can't have little cheeseburgers… but the flavor is still AMAZING!

Week 7

7

Green: Baked Ham with Hot Sweet Mustard, Garlic Mashed Potatoes and Peas

Our family rating: 9
Your family rating: _____

Yellow: Cashew Chicken on Vermicelli Pasta

Our family rating: 9.5
Your family rating: _____

Yellow: Coquille St. Jacques in Pastry with Spinach Salad

Our family rating: 10
Your family rating: _____

Blue: Chicken Mascarpone with Rice and Broccoli

Our family rating: 9.5
Your family rating: _____

Red: Cheeseburger Soup

Our family rating: 10
Your family rating: _____

Baked Ham with Hot Sweet Mustard, Garlic Mashed Potatoes and Peas

Instructions:

Take out equipment

1. Preheat **oven** to 375° F.
   Make thin slits on top of the ham. Drizzle with maple syrup, wrap completely in foil and place in preheated **oven** on an oven-safe cake pan. Set timer for 35 minutes.

   Cut an entire bulb of garlic in half. Drizzle both cut sides with oil. Wrap with foil, cut side up, and place in **oven** beside ham.

2. Wash and cut potatoes into quarters, place in large **stove-top** pot. Cover potatoes with water and bring to a full boil at high heat. Once boiling, **reduce heat** to a low boil. Set timer for 15 minutes or until you can slide a knife into the potato easily.

   …meanwhile…

3. Whisk dry mustard and vinegar together in a small **stove-top** pot. Whisk in sugar and egg yolk until combined. Cook mustard at medium heat until slightly thickened. **Remove from heat** and let stand to cool.

4. Rinse peas in colander or steamer basket. Place a small amount of water in the bottom of a **stove-top** pot and let stand.

   …when potatoes are ready…

5. Remove from heat, drain, add butter and milk, then cover to keep warm.

6. Bring water to a full boil with the peas in the basket above. Cover and set timer for 2-3 minutes...or microwave on high for 3-4 minutes, then **remove from heat** and let stand.

   …when timer rings for ham…
   Remove garlic, squeeze as many cloves as you like into the potatoes and mash with a hand masher or electric mixer.
   Serve ham with hot sweet mustard. Save half of the ham for lunches. *Our family just dies for this mustard on ham sandwiches too!!!*

Ingredients:

Take out ingredients.

ham, boneless, ready to serve, reduced-sodium (3-4 lbs or 1.3-1.8 kg)
You can set aside 2 cups, cubed ham for Ham Strata on page 152.
1 Tbsp maple syrup
aluminum foil
1 bulb garlic
1 tsp olive oil, extra-virgin

2 lbs or 900 g Yukon Gold potatoes
or thin skin potatoes (approx 6 potatoes)
The reason I use thin-skinned potatoes is so I don't have to peel them if I am in a rush… but make sure you slice off any green.
water

Hot Sweet Mustard
1/4 cup dry mustard
1/4 cup vinegar
2 Tbsp sugar
1 egg yolk

3 cups frozen baby peas

1 Tbsp butter
1/4 cup 1% milk
If you want softer potatoes you can always add a little extra milk when mashing.

If you don't use all the garlic, it is great to have as an appetizer or snack on bread or crackers—that's if it lasts that long!

Serves 4-6

DINNER IS READY IN 40 MINUTES

Equipment List:

Large stove-top pot w/lid
Small stove-top pot
Stove top pot w/steamer basket
Oven-safe cake pan
Potato masher or electric mixer
Cutting board
Colander
Sharp veggie Knife
Sharp meat knife
Whisk
Knife
Measuring cups and spoons
Aluminum foil

Per serving:

Calories	421
Fat	11.1 g
Protein	32.5 g
Carbohydrate	47.9 g
Fiber	6.6 g
Sodium	1209 mg

U.S. Food Exchanges:		Cdn. Food Choices:	
2	Starch	2 1/2	Carb
4	Meat	4 1/2	Meat/Alt
1	Vegetable	1/2	Other
1/2	Other		

Half the ham is reserved for sandwiches.

Cashew Chicken on Vermicelli Pasta

Instructions:

Don't change yet! Take out equipment.
1. Fill a large **stove-top** pot with water and bring to a boil.

2. Heat oil in a large nonstick **fry pan** or wok at medium heat. Finely chop onion, adding to pan as you cut. Add garlic.
Cut chicken into bite size pieces, adding to pan as you cut. Toss until meat is no longer pink. Cut peppers into chunks adding to pan as you cut. Wash and slice mushrooms adding to pan as you cut.

Whisk chicken broth gradually into cornstarch, so that it doesn't lump, in a medium bowl. Add curry, brown sugar, ketchup, salsa, and hot chili sauce to bowl. Stir.

Pour sauce over chicken and veggies. Stir to combine. **Reduce heat** to low and simmer until pasta is ready.

3. Place pasta in boiling water. Set timer according to package directions, approx 5 minutes.

...when timer rings...
Rinse pasta in a colander under hot water. Return to pot. Toss with olive oil if you like.

Serve pasta in bowls with sauce on top (*or in cool ceramic Chinese take out containers as shown—just kidding—but just in case you want to know, I got mine at Pottery Barn!*).

Garnish with cashews.
We also love hot chili flakes sprinkled on top.

Ingredients:

Take out ingredients.
water

1 tsp canola oil
1 onion
1 tsp garlic (from a jar)
3 chicken breasts, boneless, skinless
  (1 lb or 450 g)
1 green bell pepper
1 red bell pepper
10 mushrooms

<u>**Sauce for Chicken**</u>
1 Tbsp cornstarch
  or a little more for a thicker sauce
1 can chicken broth, reduced sodium
  (10 fl oz or 284 mL)
2 tsp curry powder
1 1/2 Tbsp brown sugar
1/2 cup ketchup
1/2 cup salsa (mild, medium or hot)
1 tsp hot chili sauce (optional)

12 oz or 340 g vermicelli pasta
  (use regular vermicelli or spaghettini, only use rice vermicelli if there are wheat allegeries in your family)

1 tsp olive oil, extra-virgin (optional)

1/3 cup cashews, unsalted or lightly salted
hot chili flakes (if you like things spicy)

<u>**Serves 4-6**</u>

DINNER IS READY IN 25 MINUTES

Equipment List:

Large stove-top pot
Large nonstick fry pan or wok
Medium mixing bowl
2 cutting boards
Colander
Sharp veggie knife
Sharp meat knife
Whisk
Serving spoon
Measuring cups and spoons

Per serving:

Calories	411
Fat	5.9 g
Protein	26.6 g
Carbohydrate	64.3 g
Fiber	2.5 g
Sodium	522 mg

U.S. Food Exchanges:		Cdn. Food Choices:	
3 1/2	Starch	3 1/2	Carb
3	Meat-lean	4	Meat/Alt
1	Vegetable	1/2	Other
1/2	Other		

20 to prep

Coquille St. Jacques in Pastry with Spinach Salad

Instructions:

Don't change yet! Take out equipment.

1. Preheat **oven** to 400° F.
Place frozen pastry shells on cookie sheet. Place in preheated **oven**. Set timer for 20 minutes or until golden brown.

2. Rinse scallops and shrimp under cold water in a colander. Remove tails from shrimp. Let stand.

Heat butter and oil in a large **stove-top** pot at medium. Finely chop white and green part of onion, adding to pot as you cut. Wash and slice mushrooms, adding to pot as you cut. **Remove from heat**. Add flour and spice, stir until the flour and spice completely coats the green onion and mushrooms.
Gradually stir in wine, cream and milk.
Return pot to **stove-top** and **reduce heat** to a low simmer.

…when timer rings for pastry…

3. Gently remove top inner disk of pastry with a fork and set aside. Remove most of the soft pastry from the inside and discard. Let cool.

4. Rinse spinach in basket of salad spinner and spin dry. Sliver red onion. Place spinach on serving plates and top with onion, frozen berries, feta and pecans. *See back flap for pecan recipe.*

Combine balsamic vinegar and maple syrup for dressing.

5. Add seafood to White Wine Sauce. **Increase heat** to medium. Stir until shrimp turn pink. Serve seafood mixture in pastry shells alongside salad.

A sprinkle of mozzarella or gruyere on each is awesome!

Ingredients:

Take out ingredients.

1 package of 6 frozen puff pastry patty shells (10 oz or 300 g)

1 lb or 450 g frozen scallops
1/2 lb or 225 g frozen shrimp, peeled and deveined

<u>White Wine Sauce</u>
1 Tbsp butter
1 Tbsp olive oil, extra-virgin
4 green onions
8 mushrooms
3 Tbsp flour
1/4 tsp salt
2 tsp parsley, dried
1/2 cup white wine
1/2 cup 10% cream
3/4 cup 1% milk

1 bag prewashed baby spinach (6 oz or 170 g)
1/8 red onion
1/2 cup frozen wild blueberries
1/4 cup feta cheese, light, crumbled (or goat cheese)
candied spiced pecans (optional)
1/4 cup balsamic salad dressing (3 parts balsamic vinegar, 2 parts maple syrup, see page 62 or use bottled)

mozzarella or gruyere cheese (optional)

<u>Serves 4-6</u>

DINNER IS READY IN 30 MINUTES

Equipment List:

Large stove-top pot
Cookie sheet
Cutting board
Colander
Salad spinner
Salad bowl
Salad tongs
Sharp veggie knife
Stirring spoon
Fork
Measuring cups and spoons

Per serving:

Calories	428
Fat	20.6 g
Protein	28.3 g
Carbohydrate	31.1 g
Fiber	1.7 g
Sodium	510 mg

U.S. Food Exchanges:		Cdn. Food Choices:	
1 1/2	Starch	1 1/2	Carb
4	Meat	4	Meat/Alt
2	Fat	2	Fat
1/2	Other	1/2	Other

20
to
prep

Chicken Mascarpone with Rice and Broccoli

Instructions:

Don't change yet! Take out equipment.

1. Heat butter and oil in a large nonstick electric or stove-top **fry pan** at medium-high. Brown chicken, smooth side down, until golden brown. Flip to slightly brown other side. Transfer chicken to a plate and set aside.

   Reduce heat to medium-low. Sliver onion, adding to uncleaned pan as you cut. Rinse and slice mushrooms, adding to pan as you cut. Add garlic and spice. Stir occasionally until onion is soft and caramelized.

   Add wine, Dijon and mascarpone to pan, stirring to combine. Return chicken to pan, rough side down, **cover** and **reduce heat** to simmer until timer rings for rice and chicken's internal temp is 170° F (approx 18 minutes). *Always use an instant read thermometer to ensure the chicken is cooked through, they are only a few bucks and really help you to know when dinner is ready.*

   ...meanwhile...

2. Combine rice and water in large microwave safe pot with lid. **Microwave** rice at high for 8 minutes, then medium for 8 minutes. A paper towel under the pot helps with any spills.

3. Rinse broccoli in colander or steamer basket. Place small amount of water in the bottom of a **stove-top** pot and bring to a full boil with the broccoli in the basket above. Cover and set timer for 3 minutes...or microwave at high for 3 minutes.

   I use an aperitif wine (Dubonnet) as it's easily available and the cost per measure is similar to other condiments. It keeps forever and you can use it for any recipe that calls for Marsala wine or port. Check out page 26 for other uses.

Ingredients:

Take out ingredients.

1 tsp butter
1 tsp olive oil, extra-virgin
10-12 chicken thighs, boneless, skinless
  (1 3/4 lbs or 800 g)

1 onion
10 mushrooms
1 Tbsp fresh garlic (from a jar)
1 tsp Italian seasoning
1 Tbsp parsley, dried
1/4 tsp fresh ground pepper

1/2 cup red aperitif wine, or Marsala wine
  or port (found in liquor store)
  I like Dubonnet because it works
  great for many recipes and is economical.
1 tsp Dijon mustard
1/2 cup mascarpone cheese
prepared cooked chicken

1 1/2 cups basmati rice
3 cups water
paper towel

1 lb or 450 g broccoli florets

Serves 4-6

DINNER IS READY IN 50 MINUTES

Equipment List:

Large nonstick electric or stove-
   top fry pan w/lid
Large microwave safe pot w/lid
Stove-top pot w/steamer basket
2 cutting boards
Colander
Sharp meat knife
Sharp veggie knife
Flipper
Stirring spoon
Plate
Instant read thermometer
Paper towel
Measuring cups and spoons

Per serving:

Calories	428
Fat	11.9 g
Protein	33.0 g
Carbohydrate	44.5 g
Fiber	1.9 g
Sodium	160 mg

U.S. Food Exchanges:		Cdn. Food Choices:	
3	Starch	3	Carb
4	Meat	5	Meat/Alt

20 to prep

Cheeseburger Soup

Instructions:

…the night before…
Take out equipment.

1. Heat oil in a large nonstick **fry pan** at medium-high. *I use my electric fry pan for this.* Sliver onion, adding to pan as you cut. Finely chop celery, adding to pan as you cut. Sauté until onion turns slightly brown, then add to inside crock of **slow cooker.**

   Reduce heat of uncleaned **fry pan** to medium. Form tiny little flat burgers (approx 1 1/2" in diameter) in the palm of your hand and brown on both sides. Once browned, add to **slow cooker**.

   …while burgers are browning…
   Add the following ingredients to **slow cooker**: spice, chili stewed tomatoes, consommé, water from both cans, pasta sauce and mixed veggies. Stir to combine. **Refrigerate** over night.

   …in the morning…
2. Set **slow cooker** at low heat. Simmer all day.

   …when ready for dinner…
3. Serve with a bowl of grated cheddar cheese at the table. Get the kids to lift their little burgers to the top of the bowl so they can sprinkle them with cheddar. *I actually find this fun!*

   Our family loves this with fresh buns, focaccia or… I make extra pasta from another meal (such as the chicken dinner this week) so that we can put a little pasta in the bottom of the bowl and pour the soup over top. Either way it's a meal in one and it is absolutely fun and delicious!!

Ingredients:

Take out ingredients.
1 tsp olive oil, extra-virgin

1 onion
2 celery ribs

1 lb or 450 g ground beef, extra-lean

1 Tbsp Italian seasoning
1/4 tsp fresh ground pepper
1/4 tsp – 1/2 tsp hot chili flakes
  (optional for spice lovers)
3 bay leaves
1 can Italian or chili stewed tomatoes
  (14 fl oz or 400 mL)
1 tomato can filled with water
1 can consommé (10 fl oz or 284 mL)
1 consommé can filled with water
1 can pasta sauce (24 fl oz or 680 mL)
  (choose a lower sodium brand)
  (or use reserved 3 cups pasta sauce from Calabrese Lasagna meal)
3 cups frozen mixed veggies

1/2 cup sharp cheddar cheese, grated, light

fresh buns or focaccia (optional)
leftover pasta (optional)

<u>Serves 6</u>

DINNER IS READY IN 25 MINUTES

Equipment List:

...the night before...
Slow cooker
Large nonstick or electric fry pan
Cutting board
Sharp veggie knife
Stirring spoon
Can opener
Measuring cups and spoons

...in the morning...
Slow cooker

...when ready for dinner...
Cheese grater
Cutting board
Bread knife
Serving spoon

Per serving:

Calories	416
Fat	12.6 g
Protein	28.7 g
Carbohydrate	50.2 g
Fiber	13.3 g
Sodium	961 mg

U.S. Food Exchanges:		Cdn. Food Choices:	
1 1/2	Starch	1 1/2	Carb
4	Meat-lean	4	Meat/Alt
1	Vegetable	1	Other
1/2	Other		

15 to prep

About the Recipes

 **Green**   Sooo easy and sooo gourmet! If you want, you can do this with raw, boneless, skinless chicken thighs or breasts or even the veggie chicken breasts. In fact, if you don't normally like veggie chicken breasts, it may be one of the few recipes you will like them in! If people in your camp don't like olives, you may be surprised how much you do in this recipe. That's what our test families say!

 **Yellow**   Every once in a while we are shocked by the test results with real families on the go! You will either loooove it….or not! We retested with brie and it did much better, but I personally die for this with gorgonzola!
Chicken or even left over steak is really nice on this for extra protein!

Blue   Soooo these may not seem that special buuuut for lamb lovers…they are the best! Lamb is expensive, so this is a way for me to get my fix during the work week! It's worth finding the mint jelly. I buy mine at Safeway. It really takes the flavor over the top!

 Yellow   Sometimes it's just nice to have a lighter dish! I always recommend when Eating Forward™ you take a look at your week and figure out which meal suits which night! When the kids were in sports and we had to have a heavier snack when we got home from work, I would whip these up once we got home. Light but delicious! Great for entertaining too!
Vegetarians who don't eat fish can smash up the same quantity of drained, canned chickpeas instead…and it's really nice!

 Yellow   Over the top! This is my all time favorite chicken burger! I'm telling you though… gorgonzola or cambozola cheese with the hot pepper jelly takes this to the next level! The crunchy with the creamy with the little bite…ooooooohh, ok, I'm salivating!
Vegetarians, the coated veggie chicken works really well!

Week 8

Green:

Mediterranean Chicken
with Rice and Asparagus

Our family rating: 9.5
Your family rating: _____

Yellow:

Pear, Brie & Caramelized Onion Tarts
with Snap Peas

Our family rating: 8
Your family rating: _____

Blue:

Lamb (or Beef) Meatballs with Fresh Mint,
Smashed Potatoes and Green Beans

Our family rating: 9.5
Your family rating: _____

Yellow:

Tuna Cakes (or Salmon or Crab)
with Raspberry & Snap Pea Salad

Our family rating: 9
Your family rating: _____

Yellow:

Spicy Crispy Chicken Burgers
with Dipping Veggies

Our family rating: 10
Your family rating: _____

Mediterranean Chicken
with Rice and Asparagus

Instructions:

...the night before...

Take out equipment.

1. Quarter chicken into two white sections (wing and breast) and two dark sections (drumstick and thigh). Place chicken into a large plastic, resealable bag.

   Sprinkle chicken with raisins and olives.

   Whisk together the following in a measuring cup: balsamic vinegar, parsley, oregano, pepper, brown sugar, olive oil and garlic. Stir until well mixed. Pour mixture over chicken in bag. Close bag tightly and let rest in bowl. **Refrigerate** overnight. Flip the bag every once in a while.

   ...when you arrive home...

2. Preheat **oven** to 350° F.

   Place chicken with marinade, skin side up, in a large oven-safe lasagna or cake pan. Place in preheated **oven**. Set timer for 20 minutes or until heated through.

3. Combine rice and water in a large microwave-safe pot with lid. **Microwave** at high for 8 minutes, then medium for 8 minutes. Place a paper towel under the rice pot in case of spillage.

4. Snap off bottom nodes of asparagus and discard. Rinse in colander or steamer basket. Place a small amount of water in the bottom of a **stove-top** pot, let stand.

   ...when timer rings for chicken...
   Bring water to full boil with asparagus in the basket above. Cover and set timer for 4 minutes...or microwave for the same amount of time. Add butter if you must.

Ingredients:

Take out ingredients.

1 whole precooked roaster chicken (2 lbs or 900 g) (assumes 1 lb or 450 g of actual meat)
large plastic resealable bag

1/2 cup raisins
1/3 cup green pimento olives, sliced (or any sliced, pitted olive of choice)
1/4 cup balsamic vinegar
1 Tbsp parsley, dried
1 Tbsp oregano
1/4 tsp fresh ground pepper
2 Tbsp brown sugar
2 Tbsp olive oil, extra-virgin
1 Tbsp fresh garlic (from a jar) (or 3 cloves, minced)

prepared chicken with marinade

1 1/2 cups basmati rice
3 cups water
paper towel

20 asparagus spears (1 lb or 450 g)

butter (optional)

<u>Serves 4-6</u>

DINNER IS READY IN 40 MINUTES

Equipment List:

...the night before...
Cutting board
Sharp meat knife
Large plastic resealable bag
Bowl
Whisk
Measuring cups and spoons

...when you arrive home...
Large oven-safe lasagna or cake
  pan
Stove-top pot w/steamer basket
Large microwave-safe pot w/lid
Colander
Measuring cups and spoons
Paper towel

Per serving:

Calories	410
Fat	11.0 g
Protein	24.1 g
Carbohydrate	54.3 g
Fiber	3.7 g
Sodium	133 mg

U.S. Food Exchanges:		Cdn. Food Choices:	
2 1/2	Starch	2 1/2	Carb
3	Meat	3	Meat/Alt
1/2	Fat	1/2	Fat
1	Other	1	Other

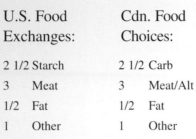

15 to prep

WEEK 8

Pear, Brie & Caramelized Onion Tarts with Snap Peas

Instructions:

…the night before…

1. Remove pastry from freezer and **refrigerate**.

…when you arrive home…

2. Remove pastry from fridge and let stand at room temperature.
Preheat **oven** to 375° F.

3. Heat oil in a large nonstick **fry pan** or wok at medium. Sliver onion, adding to pan as you cut. Stir occasionally until very soft, caramelized and slimy, approx 8 minutes. **Remove from heat.** *If you need more protein in your meal, now is the time to cut up a little chicken breast and sauté in pan.*

4. Unroll both sheets of pastry and fold each in half to create 2 tart bases approx 6" x 10". Place on cookie sheet. *If using puff pastry blocks, you will need to dust surface with flour and roll out each square with a rolling pin or wine bottle to approx the same size.*
Evenly distribute caramelized onion on each base. Wash and slice pear into thin wedges and layer on top of onion. Cut brie wheel in half, then sliver. Layer onto each tart.
Wash and finely chop green onions, scatter on top of each tart.
Place in preheated **oven** for 25 minutes or until crust shows visible layers and is golden brown.

….meanwhile…

5. Heat a large nonstick **fry pan** or wok at medium-high. Place almonds into dry pan and toss until just brown. **Remove from heat.**
Rinse snap peas in a colander and add to pan.
….when timer rings for tarts…
Drizzle peas with sesame oil and **increase heat** to high. Toss and heat through until hot, approx 2 minutes, while slicing your tarts!

Ingredients:

2 sheets frozen puff pastry (16 oz or 450 g)
You can also use 2 puff pastry blocks.

2 sheets puff pastry, unfrozen

1 tsp olive oil, extra-virgin
1 large sweet white onion

2 chicken breasts (optional)

2 sheets puff pastry, room temp

flour (optional)

prepared caramelized onion
1-2 pears
4 oz or 125 g brie *We love cambozola cheese instead of brie, your choice.*
4 green onions

1/4 cup matchstick almonds

1 lb or 450 g snap peas

1/2 tsp sesame oil

Serves 4-6

DINNER IS READY IN 30 MINUTES

Equipment List:

2 large nonstick fry pans or woks
Cutting board
Colander
Sharp veggie knife
2 stirring spoons
Rolling pin
  (if using block pastry)
Measuring cups and spoons

Per serving:

Calories	482
Fat	28.4 g
Protein	13.5 g
Carbohydrate	43.5 g
Fiber	6.0 g
Sodium	365 mg

U.S. Food Exchanges:		Cdn. Food Choices:	
2	Starch	2 1/2	Carb
1 1/2	Meat-high fat	2	Meat/Alt
3	Fat	4 1/2	Fat
1/2	Fruit		

W
E
E
K

8

Lamb (or Beef) Meatballs with Fresh Mint, Smashed Potatoes and Green Beans

Instructions:

Don't change yet! Take out equipment.

1. Wash potatoes and cut into quarters. Place in a large **stove-top** pot filled with cold water. Bring to a boil, then **reduce heat** to a low boil. Set timer for 10 minutes or until a knife can pierce the largest potato easily, then **remove from heat.**

2. Heat a large nonstick **fry pan** at medium. Form meatballs (approx 3/4" in diameter), adding to pan as your form. Brown on all sides. Sprinkle with pepper.

   …meanwhile…
   Sliver onion finely, adding to meatball pan as you cut. Rinse and slice mushrooms, adding to pan as you cut. Scatter in between meatballs.

   Gently stir in soup. Gradually add milk to pan. Add Worcestershire sauce.

   Coarsely chop mint and add to pan. Stir gently, bring to a boil then cover. **Reduce heat** and simmer for 10 minutes.

   …when timer rings for potatoes…

3. Rinse green beans in colander or steamer basket. Place a small amount of water in the bottom of a **stove-top** pot with beans in the basket above. Bring beans to a full boil. Cover and set timer for 3 minutes...or microwave at high for 3 minutes. Toss with butter if you must.

4. Drain potatoes and return to pot, **no heat**. Add butter and milk. Smash with a hand masher or electric mixer or leave whole.

   Lamb meatballs are usually served with mango chutney. However, we like to serve the meatballs with warmed mint jelly and fresh mint leaves scattered on top instead. Yum, yum, yum!

Ingredients:

Take out ingredients.
2 lbs or 900 g potatoes, thin skin or baby potatoes
When I need to save time I just use baby potatoes, they are hassle free!
water

1 lb or 450 g ground lamb or beef
1/4 tsp fresh ground pepper

1 onion or 1/2 large
10 mushrooms

1 can cream of mushroom soup, reduced-sodium (10 fl oz or 284 mL)
1/2 soup can of 1% milk
1 Tbsp Worcestershire sauce
10 fresh mint leaves (approx 3 Tbsp)

4 cups frozen green beans

butter (optional)

1 Tbsp butter
1/4 cup 1% milk

1 1/2 Tbsp mint jelly (optional)
or mango chutney as shown
fresh mint leaves (extra for garnish)

Serves 4-6

DINNER IS READY IN 40 MINUTES

Equipment List:

Large stove-top pot
Stove-top pot w/steamer basket
Large nonstick fry pan w/lid
Cutting board
Colander
Potato peeler
Potato masher or electric mixer
Sharp veggie knife
Can opener
Stirring spoon
Knife
Flipper
Measuring cups and spoons

Per serving:

Calories	470
Fat	21.1 g
Protein	20.8 g
Carbohydrate	51.8 g
Fiber	5.8 g
Sodium	313 mg

U.S. Food Exchanges:		Cdn. Food Choices:	
2	Starch	3	Carb
2	Meat-high fat	3	Meat/Alt
1	Fat	2 1/2	Fat
1	Vegetable		
1	Milk		

20 to prep

Tuna Cakes (or Salmon or Crab) with Raspberry & Snap Pea Salad

Instructions:

Don't change yet! Take out equipment.

1. Heat oil in a large nonstick **fry pan** or wok at med-high. Sliver onions finely, adding to pan as you cut. (See page 34 for how to cut an onion.) Add garlic. Stir occasionally until soft and caramelized. **Remove from heat.**

2. Slice bread into very small cubes and place in a large mixing bowl. Add egg whites, mayonnaise and Dijon mustard. Drain tuna and crumble into bowl. Add pepper and lime juice. Finely chop cilantro and add to mixing bowl. Stir in onions and garlic until completely combined.

    Divide mixture into 6 parts, form each part into a cake like a hamburger patty and **refrigerate** (this is **important**, it helps the patties hold together better when cooking).

    Combine mayonnaise and sweet chili sauce in a small mixing bowl. Set aside.

    ...meanwhile...

3. Rinse lettuce in basket of salad spinner and spin dry. Transfer lettuce to individual serving plates. Sliver onion and sprinkle over lettuce. Top with raspberries, goat cheese and pecans. *See back flap for pecan recipe.* Rinse snap peas and place alongside salad. Drizzle with salad dressing.

4. Spray a large nonstick **fry pan** with cooking spray at medium heat. Brown cakes for 3 to 5 minutes per side.

    Serve alongside salad. Drizzle with sauce. *YUM!*

Ingredients:

Take out ingredients.
1 tsp olive oil, extra-virgin
2 onions (or 1 large onion)
1 Tbsp fresh garlic (from a jar)

6 slices bread (whole wheat, frozen)
2 egg whites (save a yolk for Spicy, Crispy Chicken Burgers on page 134)
1/3 cup mayonnaise, light
  (only 1/4 cup if using crab or salmon)
2 Tbsp Dijon mustard
2 cans tuna, salmon or crab, in water
  (6 1/2 oz or 184 g each)
1/2 tsp fresh ground pepper
2 tsp lime juice
1-2 small handfuls cilantro
  (1/4 - 1/2 cup)

<u>**Sauce for Tuna Cakes**</u>
3 Tbsp mayonnaise, light
3 Tbsp sweet Thai chili sauce

1 bag mixed salad greens (6 oz or 170 g)
1/8 red onion
1/2 cup raspberries
1/4 cup goat cheese
  (or feta cheese, light, crumbled)
candied spiced pecans (optional)
1 cup snap peas
1/3 cup Vidalia onion, light, salad dressing
  (or your favorite)

cooking spray

<u>**Serves 4-6**</u>

Equipment List:

2 large nonstick fry pans or woks
Small mixing bowl
Large mixing bowl
Salad spinner
Cutting board
Colander
Can opener
Sharp veggie knife
Sharp bread knife
Bread knife
2 stirring spoons
Measuring cups and spoons

Per serving:

Calories	318
Fat	13.4 g
Protein	22.1 g
Carbohydrate	27.7 g
Fiber	4.6 g
Sodium	772 mg

U.S. Food Exchanges:		Cdn. Food Choices:	
1	Starch	1	Carb
3	Meat	3	Meat/Alt
1	Fat	1	Fat
1	Vegetable	1/2	Other
1/2	Other		

20 to prep

Spicy Crispy Chicken Burgers
with Dipping Veggies

Instructions:

Don't change yet! Take out equipment.

1. Preheat **oven** to 350° F.

2. Rinse cucumber, snap peas, celery, tomatoes and carrots. Cut celery into sticks and slice cucumber. Arrange veggies on a serving plate for people to munch on while you're making the burgers.
   You can put out a little ranch dip if you like.

3. Place buns in preheated **oven. Turn oven off.**

4. Rinse lettuce leaves and tomatoes. Slice tomatoes and sliver onion. Set aside as toppings for chicken burgers.

5. Whisk egg white in a small bowl until frothy.

   Place panko flakes on a sheet of waxed paper.
   If your family likes spicy food, you can also add cayenne or chipotle seasoning to the panko flakes.

   Drop approx 1/2 tsp oil in four separate spots in a nonstick electric **fry pan**, smear to size of cutlet. Heat oil at medium.

   Dunk each chicken cutlet into the egg white then panko flakes, coating both sides. Place flat side down in **fry pan** on oil. Partly cover with lid and flip when cutlet is golden brown (approx 4 minutes). Brown other side until internal temp is 170° F. One side will look nicer, serve that side up. *Always use an instant read thermometer to ensure the chicken is cooked through, they are only a few bucks and really help you to know when dinner is ready.*

6. Remove warm buns from **oven.**
   Spread cambozola cheese on one side of the bun and red pepper jelly on the other.
   This burger is unforgettable buuuut if you don't think your family will like cambozola or red pepper jelly, you can change them up with cream cheese and apple jelly!

Ingredients:

Take out ingredients.

1 English cucumber
1 cup snap peas
2 celery ribs
8-12 cherry tomatoes
1 lb or 450 g baby carrots
ranch dressing, light, for dip (optional)

4-6 hamburger buns, multigrain

2 cups lettuce leaves
2 tomatoes
1/4 red onion

1 egg white

1 cup panko flakes (found near coating mixes) (or cornflake crumbs)
waxed paper
cayenne or chipotle pepper (optional)

2 tsp canola oil

4 chicken cutlets (1 1/3 lbs or 600 g) (or butterflied chicken breasts as shown) See page 35 for how to butterfly chicken.
prepared egg white
panko flakes on waxed paper
   After dunking cutlets expect to have some panko flakes leftover.

1 1/2 Tbsp cambozola cheese for all (or cream cheese)
2 Tbsp red pepper jelly for all (found near gourmet condiments) or use apple jelly

Serves 4-6

DINNER IS READY IN 30 MINUTES

Equipment List:

Nonstick electric fry pan w/lid
Small mixing bowl
Baking pan
Cutting board
Colander
Sharp veggie knife
Sharp bread knife
Serving plate
Whisk
Flipper
Butter knife
Instant read thermometer
Waxed paper
Measuring cups and spoons

Per serving:

Calories	394
Fat	6.9 g
Protein	32.7 g
Carbohydrate	52.1 g
Fiber	6.3 g
Sodium	414 mg

U.S. Food Exchanges:		Cdn. Food Choices:	
2 1/2	Starch	2 1/2	Carb
4	Meat-lean	5	Meat
1	Vegetable	1/2	Other
1/2	Other		

2 Tbsp panko flakes are left over.

20 to prep

About the Recipes

Yellow   I know this is so basic, but really nice to have as a meal in the week! What is it about spaghetti and meatballs? …and then with cheese and baking it…oh my gosh!
If you have a smaller family I suggest you make two small pans and freeze one for an emergency meal on hand!
Vegetarians, store bought falafels are a great meatball replacement!

Blue   This meal is such a great entertaining dish! The little, tiny bit of sausage really makes a plain old chicken breast special! I love that it all bakes at the same time with the potatoes and veggies. Try the beets, even if you don't normally like beets. You may be pleasantly surprised when they are roasted aaaaand they are so good for you!

Yellow   Ron and I go to this one restaurant sometimes for a lunch date and it's always packed. It's all about a soup that has a very simple broth, but is loaded with veggies. We like it, but every time we go, we do wish it was spicier. I also love a hot and sour soup, but always miss the veggies, so I combined the two! If you would rather have a non-spicy version…use two cartons of chicken broth instead!
Vegetarians, leave out the shrimp but you will need more protein!

Red   I have always said, "Flank (or skirt) steak is the unsung hero of beef for stir-fry!" It's soooo tender when cut against the grain…aaaand juicy, so it's great for the grill too! This is an unusual and addicting sauce. You can also save time, as we do occasionally, and just use regular BBQ sauce on this.
Vegetarians, you can grill a portabella instead of the flank but you will need to bring your protein up. Try combining a bean mixture with fresh tomato, onion, feta and toasted pine nuts. Toss with an Italian dressing—it's a great side!

Green   This is an absolutely delicious and easy pot pie! We like to do individual onion soup bowls when entertaining or when having a special family meal. I find the pastry sheets so much easier than the blocks. I use President's Choice brand.
Vegetarians, cut up veggie chicken or use a combo of canned chickpeas and pressed tofu.

Week 9

Yellow:

Baked Spaghetti & Meatballs with Caesar Salad

Our family rating: 9.5
Your family rating: _____

Blue:

Italian Sausage-Stuffed Chicken in Dubonnet Sauce with Roasted Potatoes, Carrots & Beets

Our family rating: 9
Your family rating: _____

Yellow:

Hot and Sour Soup

Our family rating: 9
Your family rating: _____

Red:

Grilled Flank Steak with Yam Wedges and Broccoli

Our family rating: 8
Your family rating: _____

Green:

Chicken Pot Pie with a Mixed Greens Salad

Our family rating: 10
Your family rating: _____

Baked Spaghetti & Meatballs
with Caesar Salad

Instructions:

Don't change yet! Take out equipment.
1. Preheat **oven** to 375° F.

2. Fill a large **stove-top** pot with water and bring to a boil for pasta.

3. Heat a large nonstick electric or stove-top **fry pan** at medium. Form 1" meatballs, adding to pan as you form. Finely chop onion, then celery and carrots, adding to pan as you cut. Sauté until slightly soft, while meatballs are browning. Once meatballs have browned, set them aside on a plate, but leave veggies in! Add pasta sauce, water and spice to remaining veggies.

4. Place pasta in boiling water. Set timer for 2 minutes less than package directions, approx 8 minutes.
   ...meanwhile...

5. Rinse lettuce in basket of salad spinner and spin dry. Place in large bowl.

   ...when timer rings for pasta...
6. Rinse pasta in colander under hot water. Layer a small amount of sauce on the bottom of cake or lasagna pan. Top with 1/3 of the cooked noodles, sauce, ricotta cheese, Parmesan cheese and mozzarella. Repeat 2 more times, but on your last layer, scatter meatballs on top before you add the sauce and leave the layer of mozzarella cheese off. Cover with foil and place in preheated **oven**. Set timer for 25 minutes.

   ...when timer rings for baked spaghetti...
7. Toss the Romaine leaves with dressing. Add croutons, bacon bits and Parmesan.

8. Scatter the last amount of mozzarella on top of spaghetti and **broil**...watching very carefully so that it doesn't burn.

Ingredients:

Take out ingredients.

water

1 lb or 450 g ground beef, extra-lean
  (or use ground chicken)
1 onion
2 celery ribs
2 carrots
1 can tomato pasta sauce
  (24 fl oz or 680 mL) *Choose a low sodium brand to reduce your sodium intake.*
1/3 can water
1 tsp Italian seasoning

8 oz or 225 g spaghetti pasta

1 head Romaine lettuce

3 Tbsp sauce
1/3 of the cooked noodles
1/3 of the sauce
1/3 of the ricotta cheese or 1% cottage cheese (1 cup total)
1/3 of the Parmesan cheese, light, grated (1/4 cup total)
1/3 of the mozzarella cheese, part-skim, shredded (1 cup total)
repeat above ingredients 2 times
prepared meatballs (before sauce on last layer)
aluminum foil

1/3 cup of caesar dressing, fat-free or light
1/2 cup croutons
bacon bits (optional)
2 Tbsp Parmesan cheese, light, grated

1/3 mozzarella cheese
<u>Serves 6</u>

DINNER IS READY IN 30 MINUTES

Equipment List:

Large stove-top pot
Large nonstick electric or
  stove-top fry pan
Large cake or lasagna pan
Cutting board
Colander
Plate
Salad spinner
Salad bowl
Salad tongs
Sharp veggie knife
Cheese grater
Can opener
Aluminum foil
Measuring cups and spoons

Per serving:

Calories	546
Fat	18.6 g
Protein	35.3 g
Carbohydrate	57.9 g
Fiber	7.5 g
Sodium	882 mg

20
to
prep

U.S. Food Exchanges:		Cdn. Food Choices:	
2 1/2	Starch	3	Carb
4	Meat	5	Meat/Alt
1 1/2	Fat	1	Fat
1	Vegetable	1/2	Other
1/2	Other		

W
E
E
K

9

Italian Sausage-Stuffed Chicken in Dubonnet Sauce w/Roasted Potatoes, Carrots & Beets

Instructions:

Don't change yet! Take out equipment.
1. Preheat **oven** to 450° F.

2. Place rinsed carrots into a mixing bowl. Wash and cut potatoes into large chunks, adding to carrot bowl as you cut. Drizzle with olive oil and sprinkle with spice. Place on a cookie sheet with sides. Push to one side of sheet, in a single layer.

   Rinse, trim and cut beets in quarters, adding to uncleaned bowl. Drizzle with olive oil and spice. Place beets on the opposite side of pan. Place in **oven** (even if it hasn't completely preheated).

3. Make a tiny slit into the thickest part of the chicken breasts from the side. Use your thumb to make the pocket larger. Stuff approx 1 Tbsp sausage meat into each. Set aside. Heat oil in four different spots in a large nonstick **electric or stove-top** pan at medium. Smoosh each to the size of a chicken breast.

   Place egg white in a bowl and panko flakes on a sheet of waxed paper. Dunk each breast in egg then completely coat in panko. Sauté top of breast until golden and crispy (you only fry one side). Transfer to a second oven-safe pan, crispy side up and place in hot **oven** beside veggies. **Reduce heat** to 400° F. Set timer for 25 minutes or until internal temp of chicken is 170° F.

   ...meanwhile...
4. Finely chop onion adding to uncleaned **fry pan** as you cut. Rinse and slice mushrooms, adding to pan as you cut. When onion is slightly brown, **remove from heat,** stir in flour and add spice. Slowly whisk in wine and milk. Heat until slightly thickened.

   Serve Dubonnet Sauce on plate with chicken on top and veggies on the side.

Ingredients:

Take out ingredients.

2 cups baby carrots (or 4 carrots sliced in half then lengthwise)
4 potatoes, thin skin (2 lbs or 900 g)
1 tsp olive oil, extra-virgin
1/2 tsp garlic and herb seasoning, salt-free

3 beets
1/2 tsp olive oil, extra-virgin
1/8 tsp garlic and herb seasoning, salt-free

4 chicken breasts, boneless, skinless (1 1/2 lbs or 675 g)
1/4 cup hot or mild Italian sausage (for all) You can freeze the rest for Sicilian pasta.
4 tsp olive oil, extra-virgin

1 egg white
1 cup panko flakes (found near coating mixes)
waxed paper

Dubonnet Sauce
1/2 onion
6 mushrooms
   I prefer brown but you can use white.
2 tsp flour
1/8 tsp fresh ground pepper
1 tsp Dubonnet (sweet red wine found in liquor store)
3/4 cup 1% milk

Serves 4-6

DINNER IS READY IN 50 MINUTES

Equipment List:

Large nonstick electric
  or stove-top fry pan
2 medium mixing bowls
2 cookie sheets w/sides
2 cutting boards
Colander
Sharp veggie knife
Sharp meat knife
Stirring spoon
Whisk
Instant read thermometer
Measuring cups and spoons
Waxcd paper

Per serving:

Calories	473
Fat	12.5 g
Protein	37.1 g
Carbohydrate	53.2 g
Fiber	6.4 g
Sodium	340 mg

U.S. Food Exchanges:		Cdn. Food Choices:	
2 1/2	Starch	3	Carb
4 1/2	Meat	5	Meat/Alt
2	Vegetables		

20 to prep

Hot and Sour Soup

Instructions:

Don't change yet! Take out equipment.
1. Fill a large **stove-top** pot with water for pasta and let stand.

2. Heat oil in a different, large **stove-top** pot at medium-low.
Trim lemongrass on both ends so you are left with the bulb. Pound with a mallet or kitchen hammer, then finely chop. (See page 35 for illustrations.) Discard the stringy, long parts. Add the rest to pan.
Cut carrot into 4, then each quarter into 6 slivers, adding to lemongrass pot as you cut. Cut chilies in half and take the seeds out. *Wash your hands and don't rub your eyes!* Finely chop, adding to pot as you cut. Once fragrant, add water, Tom Yum paste, fish sauce, lime juice and sugar. Stir and bring to a boil.

Trim and coarsely chop white and green parts of onion, adding to pot as you cut. Finely chop cilantro, adding to pot as you cut. Rinse and cut broccoli into bite size pieces, adding to pot as you cut.
Cut tofu into strips and add to broth.
Add kaffir lime leaves. **Reduce heat** to a high simmer. Add shrimp. Set timer for 10 minutes. Soup is ready when shrimp have turned completely pink and veggies are tender.

3. Bring pasta water to a full boil. Once boiling, add pasta. Set timer according to package directions, approx 4 minutes.
…when timer rings for pasta…
Drain and rinse pasta in hot water.

Serve pasta in bottom of individual bowls. Use a slotted spoon to get your shrimp, veggies and tofu, then use a ladle to cover with broth. Garnish soup with green onion.

Ingredients:

Take out ingredients.
water

1 tsp canola oil

2 lemongrass stalks (approx 1/4 cup)
(or in a tube)

1 carrot
3 small red Thai chilies

10 cups water
1-2 Tbsp Tom Yum paste
(If you don't like spicy food, just add 1 tsp + 7–8 cups veggie or chicken broth.)
3 Tbsp fish sauce
1/4 cup lime juice
3 Tbsp brown sugar
4 green onions
1/4 cup cilantro
3 cups broccoli florets (or a combination of veggies you have on hand as shown)

6 oz or 170 g tofu, pressed
4 kaffir lime leaves (or 4 bay leaves and 1 tsp lime zest)
1 lb or 450 g shrimp, peeled and deveined (Photo shown with no shrimp option.)

6 oz or 170 g vermicelli pasta
(use regular vermicelli or spaghettini, only use rice vermicelli if there are wheat allegeries in your family)

green onion (for garnish)

<u>**Serves 4-6**</u>

DINNER IS READY IN 30 MINUTES

Equipment List:

2 large stove-top pots
Cutting board
Colander
Sharp veggie knife
Mallet or rolling pin
Stirring spoon
Slotted spoon
Ladle
Measuring cups and spoons

Per serving:

Calories	259
Fat	2.7 g
Protein	21.8 g
Carbohydrate	37.8 g
Fiber	1.2 g
Sodium	924 mg

U.S. Food Exchanges:		Cdn. Food Choices:	
2	Starch	2	Carb
3	Meat- very lean	3	Meat/Alt
1	Vegetable	1/2	Other
1/2	Other		

Grilled Flank Steak
with Yam Wedges and Broccoli

Instructions:

...the night before...

Take out equipment.

1. Prepare marinade in the bottom of a large lasagna or cake pan by combining balsamic vinegar, wine, cherry jam, oil and spice.

   Cut diagonal slits into the top of the flank (as shown) and place flank on marinade, slit side down. Cover with plastic wrap and **refrigerate**.
   Every time you happen to be in the fridge... give it a flip.

...when you get home...

2. Preheat **BBQ** or broiler to medium. Cut yams in half or quarter lengthwise, depending on size. Brush oil on flat sides of yams and place on grill, flat side down. Rotate to create nice grill marks.
   When able to pierce easily, wrap in foil to keep warm or place on side of BBQ with no direct heat.
   Increase heat to medium-high (for steak).

3. Place steak on **BBQ grill** slit side down. Grill 3 minutes then rotate (to create grill marks). Grill another 3 minutes. Flip and grill 3 final minutes. (Total grilling time is 9 minutes.) Serve slit side up, slicing meat very thinly across the grain.

...while grilling steak...

4. Rinse broccoli in colander or steamer basket. Place a small amount of water in the bottom of a **stove-top** pot and bring to a full boil with the broccoli in the basket above. Cover and set timer for 3 minutes...or microwave at high for 3 minutes.

I love to serve the yams with light sour cream and a little green onion or chives.

Ingredients:

Take out ingredients.

Marinade
2 Tbsp balsamic vinegar
2 Tbsp red wine (or Dubonnet, sweet red wine found in liquor store)
1 Tbsp cherry jam (or raspberry)
1 tsp sesame oil
1/2 tsp garlic powder
1 tsp five spice powder
1/2 tsp fresh ground pepper
1/2 tsp hot chili flakes (optional)
1 1/2 lbs or 675 g flank or skirt steak
plastic wrap

6 yams (long and skinny)
 (1 1/2-2 lbs or 675-900 g)
 (Not a large sweet potato. If using a large sweet potato, cut lengthwise into 4-6 long, skinny wedges.)
aluminum foil

1 lb or 450 g broccoli florets

sour cream, light (optional)
green onion (optional)

Serves 4-6

DINNER IS READY IN 25 MINUTES

Equipment List:

…the night before…
Large lasagna or cake pan
Sharp meat knife
Plastic wrap
Measuring cups and spoons

…when you get home…
Broiler pan or BBQ grill
Stove-top pot w/steamer basket
Cutting board
Colander
Sharp veggie knife
Pastry brush
Fork
BBQ tongs
Aluminum foil

Per serving:

Calories	352
Fat	9.3 g
Protein	28.1 g
Carbohydrate	38.8 g
Fiber	4.8 g
Sodium	93 mg

U.S. Food Exchanges:	Cdn. Food Choices:
2 1/2 Starch	2 1/2 Carb
3 1/2 Meat	4 Meat/Alt

15 to prep

W
E
E
K

9

Chicken Pot Pie with a Mixed Greens Salad

Instructions:

...the night before...

1. Take out 1 sheet of frozen puff pastry and place in **refrigerator** to defrost overnight.

...when you get home...

2. Preheat **oven** to 400° F.

3. Heat oil in a large **stove-top** pot at medium. Finely chop onion, adding to pot as you cut. Stir occasionally until soft and caramelized. Rinse and slice celery into small pieces, adding to pot as you cut. Rinse and slice mushrooms, adding to pot as you cut. Cut chicken into bite size pieces, adding to pot as you cut. Stir until meat is no longer pink.

Add spice, soup and water. Stir to combine.

Cut broccoli into bite size pieces, adding to pot as you cut. Add frozen veggies and stir. Pour into a 10 cup casserole dish. *Oooor for a fancier look, pour into oven-safe onion soup bowls as shown!*

4. Unroll and stretch pastry sheet to drape dish, leaving a couple vents on the side. *Remember, if it's not perfect it looks even better, so don't obsess!* Place on middle rack in **oven**. Set timer for 20 minutes or until pastry is golden brown.

...meanwhile...

5. Rinse greens in basket of salad spinner and spin dry, place in bowl. Slice pepper into strips and sliver onion. Layer salad with toppings and drizzle with dressing.

Ingredients:

1 sheet frozen puff pastry (8 oz or 225 g)
You can also use a block of pastry.

1 tsp canola or olive oil, extra-virgin
1 onion

2 celery ribs
10 mushrooms
**3 chicken breasts, boneless, skinless
(1 lb or 450 g)**

1 tsp lemon pepper, salt-free
1 tsp Italian seasoning
1/4 tsp fresh ground pepper
1/4 tsp garlic and herb seasoning, salt-free
1 can cream of celery soup
(or use cream of chicken) **(10 fl oz or
284 mL)**
1 soup can filled with water
2 cups broccoli florets (1/2 lb or 225 g)
1 cup frozen mixed veggies

**1 sheet thawed puff pastry
(8 oz or 225 g)**
If using a block instead of of a sheet, you will need to dust the counter with flour and roll it out with a rolling pin or wine bottle to the size of the pan you are using.

6 oz or 170 g mixed salad greens, prewashed
1/2 red bell pepper
1/8 red onion
1/4 cup vinaigrette dressing, fat-free

Serves 4-6

DINNER IS READY IN 40 MINUTES

Equipment List:

Large stove-top pot
10 cup casserole dish
2 cutting boards
Colander
Salad spinner
Salad bowl
Salad tongs
Sharp veggie knife
Sharp meat knife
Stirring spoon
Can opener
Rolling pin
 (if using block pastry)
Measuring cups and spoons

Per serving:

Calories	376
Fat	14.8 g
Protein	26.2 g
Carbohydrate	35.8 g
Fiber	6.1 g
Sodium	767 mg

U.S. Food Exchanges:		Cdn. Food Choices:	
1 1/2	Starch	2	Carb
3 1/2	Meat	4	Meat/Alt
1	Fat	1/2	Fat
2	Vegetable		

About the Recipes

Green

This is amazing! It's ok to leave the skin on the chicken sometimes! When you are Eating Forward™ and know what you are having for dinner that night, you simply adjust your fat intake in the day and ENJOY! This combo is really nice. Although you can replace the fig jam with a different jam, such as apricot or peach, it's worth finding the fig jam or preserves!

Blue

I was pleasantly surprised when the test families gave this recipe a big thumbs up! We weren't sure if families would go for it, but their feedback was just what we were hoping! The night before makes it convenient…great as well for a pot-luck or a nice brunch! Our kids love this and I think your kids will too!
Vegetarians, don't put the ham in and make up for it with an extra 2 cups asparagus or another green vegetable such as broccoli.

Red

This is such a cool way to have perogies! I like perogies the traditional ways as well, but this is an easy, filling and delicious alternative that the whole family will love! Vegetarians, use veggie chicken.

Yellow

I just love this steak sandwich! It's one of those feel good meals with a twist! Vegetarians, try a grilled portabella instead of steak! Do everything else the same, it's really good!

Red

Very gourmet! Ron and I love having this on date night! It has a really interesting combination of flavors. It also works really well with shrimp if scallops aren't your thing! We also tried this with the tiny bay scallops, which are less expensive, but it was just ok!
Vegetarians, we found the deep fried tofu cubes worked really nice!

Week 10

Green: Roasted Fig & Pesto Chicken
with Baby Potatoes and Asparagus

Our family rating: 10
Your family rating: _____

Blue: Ham Strata with Greek Salad

Our family rating: 8.5
Your family rating: _____

Red: Chicken-Fajita Perogies

Our family rating: 9
Your family rating: _____

Yellow: Steak Sandwich with Chipotle Mayo,
Spinach Salad and Corn

Our family rating: 10
Your family rating: _____

Red: Smoked Canadian Bacon, Scallops,
Apples & Zucchini on Rice

Our family rating: 9
Your family rating: _____

Roasted Fig & Pesto Chicken with Baby Potatoes and Asparagus

Instructions:

Don't change yet! Take out equipment.
1. Preheat **oven** to 450° F.

2. Wash potatoes and place in a small oven-safe pan on middle rack. Drizzle with olive oil and sprinkle with spice. Toss potatoes until well coated. Place in oven (don't wait for oven to preheat).

...meanwhile...

3. Combine fig jam and pesto in a small mixing bowl.

Lift skin of each chicken breast and spread 1/4 of the mixture under each skin. Sprinkle tops of chicken breast with pepper.

Reduce heat to 400° F.
Place chicken in a different oven-safe pan and place in **oven** beside potatoes. *You can use 1 large pan for both as well.*
Set timer for 35 minutes or until internal temperature is 170° F in the thickest part of chicken.

4. Snap off bottom nodes of asparagus and discard. Rinse in colander or steamer basket. Place a small amount of water in the bottom of a **stove-top** pot. Let stand.

...just before chicken and potatoes are ready...
Bring water to a full boil with the asparagus in the basket above. Cover and set timer for 4 minutes...or microwave for the same amount of time. Drain water. Toss in pot with butter and salt, if you must!

...when timer rings...
Serve chicken alongside potatoes and asparagus. *Yummmm!*

If you want to make the chicken ahead for company, it freezes beautifully raw.

Ingredients:

Take out ingredients.

20 baby potatoes (2 lbs or 900 g)
(or 4 large, cut into chunks) (if baby potatoes are large, cut in half)
1 tsp olive oil, extra-virgin
1/2 tsp original, all purpose seasoning, salt-free

1 Tbsp fig jam
If you don't want to add fig jam to your pantry, you can use a peach preserve.
2 Tbsp basil pesto
4 chicken breasts with skin, bone in (1 3/4 lb or 800 g)
1/2 tsp fresh ground pepper for all

Always use an instant read thermometer to ensure the chicken is cooked through, they are only a few bucks and really help you to know when dinner is ready.

20 asparagus spears (1 lb or 450 g)
water

butter (optional)
1/2 tsp salt (optional)

<u>Serves 4-6</u>

DINNER IS READY IN 55 MINUTES

Equipment List:

2 oven-safe pans
Stove-top pot w/steamer basket
Small mixing bowl
Cutting board
Colander
Stirring spoon
Sharp veggie knife
Sharp meat knife
Instant read thermometer
Measuring cups and spoons

Per serving:

Calories	367
Fat	13.9 g
Protein	29.2 g
Carbohydrate	31.8 g
Fiber	5.0 g
Sodium	117 mg

U.S. Food Exchanges:		Cdn. Food Choices:	
2	Starch	2	Carb
3 1/2	Meat-lean	4	Meat/Alt
1	Fat	1/2	Fat

1/4 lb of chicken is bone and excess skin.

Ham Strata with Greek Salad

Instructions:

...the night before...
Take out equipment.

1. Cut ham into cubes and set aside. Snap off bottom nodes of asparagus and discard. Rinse in colander. Slice asparagus into approx 1" peices. Set aside.

2. Spray a large lasagna or cake pan with cooking spray. Layer in this order: 1/3 each of ham, bread cubes, asparagus and cheese. Repeat to make 3 layers.
Finely chop onion and sprinkle over top.

   Whisk eggs whites in a mixing bowl until frothy. Add in yolks, milk and mustard and whisk again. Pour evenly over casserole. Cover and **refrigerate** overnight (or at least a couple of hours in advance).

...when you get home...
3. Preheat **oven** to 350° F.
Uncover casserole and bake in preheated oven. Set timer for 50 minutes.

...while Ham Strata is baking...
4. Wash and cut tomatoes, green pepper and cucumber into chunks, placing in a large serving bowl as you cut. Sliver onion and crumble feta, add to bowl. Smash garlic then finely chop. Add garlic and olives to bowl.

   Sprinkle with spice then drizzle with olive oil, lemon juice and red wine vinegar. Toss to coat. Set aside until ready to serve.

Ingredients:

Take out ingredients.

2 cups cooked ham, low-sodium
  (1/2 lb or 225 g ham steak) or use reserved ham from Ham Dinner on page 114
7 asparagus spears (1/3 lb or 150 g)
  (or small broccoli florets)

cooking spray
prepared cubed ham
5 cups dried bread cubes, whole wheat
  (found in Bakery section near large bread crumbs)
cut asparagus
2 cups cheddar cheese, light, shredded
1/2 onion
6 eggs
2 1/2 cups 1% milk
1 tsp dry mustard

3 Roma tomatoes
1 green bell pepper
1/2 English cucumber
1/4 red onion
1/2 cup feta cheese, light, crumbled
1 clove garlic, minced (or 1 tsp from a jar)
1/2 cup black olives (optional)
1/2 tsp lemon pepper, salt-free
1 tsp oregano leaves
1/2 tsp thyme leaves
2 Tbsp olive oil, extra-virgin
1 Tbsp lemon juice
1 tsp red wine vinegar (or balsamic vinegar)

Serves 6-8

DINNER IS READY IN 60 MINUTES

Equipment List:

...the night before...
Large lasagna or cake pan
Mixing bowl
Cutting board
Colander
Sharp knife for meat and veggies
Whisk
Cheese grater
Measuring cups and spoons
...when you get home...
Cutting board
Colander
Salad bowl
Salad tongs
Sharp veggie knife
Measuring cups and spoons

Per serving:

Calories	437
Fat	16.8 g
Protein	28.2 g
Carbohydrate	43.0 g
Fiber	2.7 g
Sodium	790 mg

U.S. Food Exchanges:		Cdn. Food Choices:	
2 1/2	Starch	2 1/2	Carb
4	Meat	4	Meat/Alt
1	Fat	1	Fat
1	Vegetable	1/2	Other

20 to prep

Chicken-Fajita Perogies

Instructions:

Don't change yet! Take out equipment.

1. Heat oil and butter in a nonstick **electric fry pan** or **stove-top** pot at medium-low. Finely chop onion, adding to pan as you cut.

   Add frozen perogies to onion pan and brown on one side then flip to brown other side (approx 2 minutes per side).

2. **Increase heat** to medium-high.
   Cut chicken into bite size pieces, adding to pan as you cut. Scatter chicken around perogies. Rinse and slice mushrooms, adding to pan as you cut. Coarsely chop peppers, adding to pan as you cut. Slice zucchini into bite size pieces, adding to pan as you cut. Stir. Add salsa and water.

   Cover and **reduce heat** to medium-low. Set timer for 10 minutes.

   …while perogies are cooking…
   Rinse and cut tomato. Place toppings in small serving bowls. Take out anything else you would normally have with fajitas.

   I was never much of a perogie fan until I created these!! Yuuuummmy! The kid in you, as well as the kids, will love them!

Ingredients:

Take out ingredients.
1 tsp olive oil, extra-virgin
1 tsp butter
1 onion

20 perogies (1 1/3 lb or 600 g)
We use potato and onion perogies.

3 chicken breasts, boneless, skinless
 (1 lb or 450 g) *Our test families thought sausage meat might be nice as well.*
8 mushrooms
1/4 green bell pepper
1/4 red bell pepper
1 zucchini
1 cup chunky salsa (mild, medium or hot)
1/2 cup water

Toppings
1 Roma tomato
1/2 cup sour cream, light
1/4 cup tortilla chips
 (a few to crush on top)
1/2 cup Romaine lettuce, shredded
2-3 green onions

Serves 4-6

DINNER IS READY IN 25 MINUTES

Equipment List:

Electric fry pan or stove-top pot
  w/lid
2 cutting boards
Colander
Sharp veggie knife
Sharp meat knife
Flipper
Stirring spoon
Small serving bowls
Measuring cups and spoons

Per serving:

Calories	384
Fat	8.5 g
Protein	26.3 g
Carbohydrate	52.6 g
Fiber	4.6 g
Sodium	718 mg

U.S. Food Exchanges:		Cdn. Food Choices:	
3	Starch	3	Carb
3	Meat	4	Meat/Alt
1	Vegetable	1/2	Other

15 to prep

Steak Sandwich with Chipotle Mayo, Spinach Salad and Corn

Instructions:

Don't change yet! Take out equipment.

1. Combine mayonnaise, spice and pesto in a small bowl. Set aside.

2. Preheat **BBQ** to medium.

3. Heat oil in a small nonstick **fry pan** or wok at medium-high. Sliver shallot, adding to pan as you cut. Add garlic. Rinse and slice mushrooms, adding to pan as you cut. Sauté for 2-3 minutes then **remove from heat.** Set aside on plate covered in foil.

4. Rinse spinach leaves in basket of salad spinner, spin dry and place on dinner plates. Cut mango into cubes and scatter over spinach. Sliver onion and layer on spinach. Sprinkle with goat cheese and nuts then drizzle with dressing just before serving.

5. Place steak on **BBQ** for approx 3 minutes. Rotate steak clockwise for a couple minutes to create grill marks, then flip steak to other side. Slightly undercook steaks to your preference then transfer to a plate and wrap in foil. Steak keeps cooking while resting (see page 32).

   ...meanwhile...

6. Place corn on grill once steak has been rotated. While steak is cooking, make sure you turn the corn to create that smoky flavor all over.

7. Slice French loaf in half lengthwise and place only half on grill, open side down, for just a minute or two.
   Cut the loaf into 4-6 equal parts.

   To serve, either drizzle chipotle mayo on top of steak, or on the bun under the steak, you decide! Cover with mushroom mixture. Serve alongside corn and salad. Simple but really yummy!

Ingredients:

Take out ingredients.
Chipotle Mayo
1/4 cup mayonnaise, light
1/2 tsp S.W. chipotle seasoning, salt-free
1/8 tsp chipotle pepper
  (or more, if you like it spicier)
1 tsp tomato pesto (or basil pesto)

1 tsp olive oil, extra-virgin
1 shallot (or 3 green onions)
2 tsp fresh garlic (from a jar)
10 mushrooms
aluminum foil

6 oz or 170 g prewashed baby spinach
1/2 mango
1/8 red onion
1/4 cup goat cheese or feta, light, crumbled
1/4 cup nuts, such as pecans (optional)
1/4 cup vinaigrette dressing for all, fat free

1 1/2 lbs or 675 g sirloin steak, trimmed, 1 1/2" to 2" thick

aluminum foil

2 cobs of corn, cut in half (or 4 small)

French loaf (only half - freeze the other half)
I even butter the one I am freezing and sprinkle it with garlic powder and parsley so that I have garlic bread at my fingertips.

Serves 4-6

DINNER IS READY IN 25 MINUTES

Equipment List:

BBQ grill
Small nonstick fry pan or wok
Small mixing bowl
Salad spinner
Cutting board
Colander
Plate
Sharp veggie knife
Sharp bread knife
Measuring cups and spoons
Aluminum foil

Per serving:

Calories	535
Fat	25.5 g
Protein	42.3 g
Carbohydrate	33.4 g
Fiber	3.4 g
Sodium	606 mg

U.S. Food Exchanges:		Cdn. Food Choices:	
2	Starch	2	Carb
5	Meat	6	Meat/Alt
2	Fat	2	Fat
1	Vegetable		

Smoked Canadian Bacon, Scallops, Apples & Zucchini on Rice

Instructions:

Don't change yet! Take out equipment.

1. Combine rice and water in large microwave-safe pot with lid. **Microwave** at high for 8 minutes, stir, then medium for 8 minutes. Place a paper towel under pot for any spills.

   …meanwhile…

2. Heat butter and oil in a large nonstick **fry pan** at medium-low.
   Pat scallops with a paper towel and place in pan. Sauté just until golden brown then flip to other side and brown. Set aside on plate. Cover with foil to keep warm.

   Sliver bacon into thin strips and sauté in uncleaned pan at medium. Slice zucchini with skin into disks, adding to pan as you cut. Cut apple with skin into quarters. Trim core from each then sliver each quarter, adding to pan as you cut. Add spice. Sauté until just brown then add to scallop plate. Cover with same foil.

   Pour apple juice, lemon juice, hot pepper sauce and soy sauce into the uncleaned pan. When sauce begins to boil, **reduce heat** to simmer. Simmer until sauce is reduced to about half.

   Return scallops, bacon, zucchini and apple to pan. Gently stir to combine and let simmer an additional 5 minutes.

   Serve on hot rice, yuuuummmy!

   This meal is a little more expensive so definitely a treat or entertaining meal. Really, really good especially if you are a scallop nut!

Ingredients:

Take out ingredients.
1 1/2 cups basmati rice
3 cups water

paper towel

1 Tbsp butter
1 Tbsp olive oil, extra-virgin
1 lb or 450 g scallops
   The larger the scallop, the better the flavor, so avoid the real tiny ones. If purchasing frozen scallops, defrost. *For a heartier meal you can also add shrimp.*
paper towel
aluminum foil

6 slices Canadian back bacon
   (6 oz or 170 g)
1 zucchini (or 2 small)
2 Spartan apples
2 tsp sage leaves
1 tsp hot pepper seasoning (such as Club House Hot Shot or any hot pepper blend) Use a smaller amount if you want less bite.

Apple Juice Reduction
1 1/3 cup apple juice, unsweetened
2 tsp lemon juice
1/2 tsp hot pepper sauce
1/4 tsp soy sauce, reduced-sodium

Serves 4-6

DINNER IS READY IN 25 MINUTES

Equipment List:

Large microwave-safe pot w/lid
Large nonstick fry pan
2 cutting boards
Sharp veggie knife
Sharp meat knife
Flipper
Plate
Measuring cups and spoons
Paper towel
Aluminum foil

Per serving:

Calories	358
Fat	7.4 g
Protein	22.1 g
Carbohydrate	49.9 g
Fiber	2.3 g
Sodium	562 mg

U.S. Food Exchanges:		Cdn. Food Choices:	
3	Starch	3	Carb
2 1/2	Meat	3	Meat/Alt
1/2	Fruit	1/2	Other

15
to
prep

EAT SHEETS ™

RECIPE NAME	Page
Mole Chicken, Rice, Broccoli	42
Calabrese Lasagna, Spinach Salad	44
Beef and Bok Choy on Vermicelli Pasta	46
Crispy Lemon Chicken, Rice, Snap Peas	48
Raspberry-Maple Ribs, Sweet Potato, Celery	50

MEATS

Chicken thighs, boneless, skinless (10-12)
(1 3/4 lbs or 800 g)
Chicken cutlets (or butterflied breasts) (4)
 (1 1/2 lbs or 675 g)
Flank steak (or skirt or sirloin) (1 1/2 lbs or 675 g)
Pork ribs, lean, back or side (2 1/2 lbs or 1125 g)
Ground beef, extra-lean (1 lb or 450 g)

DAIRY

Egg white (1)
Milk, 1% milk fat
Feta cheese, light, crumbled (1/4 cup) (optional)
Cottage cheese, 1% milk fat (2 cups)
Mozzarella cheese, part-skim, shredded (2 cups)
Parmesan cheese, light, grated (1/2 cup)

PRODUCE

Fresh garlic (from a jar) or use cloves
Onion (2) for 3 meals
Green onions (2)
Red onion (optional for Spinach Salad)
Red bell pepper (1)
Green bell pepper (1/4)
Sweet potato (1 large)
 (1 1/2 to 2 lbs or 675 g to 900 g)
Baby spinach, prewashed (6 oz or 170 g)
Baby bok choy (6 or 1 large) (approx 1 lb or 450 g)
Celery ribs (6)
Snap peas (1 lb or 450 g)
Broccoli florets (1 lb or 450 g)
Mushrooms (18) for 2 meals

DRY ESSENTIALS

Basmati rice (1 1/2 cups)
Mixed rice (1 1/2 cups)
 I use Canoe brand with dehydrated veggies.
Vermicelli pasta (12 oz or 340 g)
 (use regular vermicelli or spaghettini, only
 use rice vermicelli if wheat allergies in family)
Panko flakes (1 cup) (found in coating mix aisle–
 or use fine bread crumbs–but panko is best)

SPICES

Cinnamon
Coriander
Cumin, ground
Onion flakes
Hot chili flakes (optional for Beef & Bok Choy)
Sesame seeds, toasted (optional for Mole Chicken)
Pepper

BAKING GOODS

Olive oil, extra-virgin & Canola oil
Sesame oil
Vinegar
Sugar
Cornstarch
Matchstick almonds

HELPERS

2 cans tomato pasta sauce, choose a lower sodium
 brand (24 fl oz or 680 mL each) *I like spicy.*
Chicken broth, reduced-sodium (1 1/2 cups)
Sweet Thai chili sauce
Ketchup
Salsa, chunky (mild, medium or hot) (1 1/4 cups)
Soy sauce, reduced-sodium
Liquid Smoke (found near sauces)
Kepac Manis (sweet Indonesian soy sauce)
 (or mushroom soy & honey)
Salad dressing, your favorite, fat-free
Lemon juice (1/4 cup) or use a fresh lemon
Mayonnaise, no-fat or light
Maple syrup
Raspberry jam
Peanut butter, light (or almond butter)
Chocolate syrup, *I use Quik*

FROZEN FOODS

Wild blueberries (1/4 cup)

BAKERY

1 loaf Calabrese bread (or French loaf)

OTHER

Aluminum foil
Plastic wrap
Paper towels
Waxed paper

Custom Eat Sheet™

RECIPE NAME   Page

_____

_____

_____

_____

_____

MEATS

DAIRY

PRODUCE

DRY ESSENTIALS

SPICES

BAKING GOODS

HELPERS

FROZEN FOODS

BAKERY

OTHER

RECIPE NAME	Page

MEATS

Chicken breasts, boneless, skinless (3) (1 lb or 450 g)
Chicken drumsticks (10-12) (approx 2 lbs or 900 g)
Ground beef, extra-lean (1/2 lb or 225 g)
Ground turkey (1/2 lb or 225 g)
Italian sausage meat (1/2 lb or 225 g)
  (mild, medium or hot)
Bacon strips, fully cooked, low-sodium (4)
Salmon filets, boneless, skinless (1 1/2 lbs or 675 g)

DAIRY

Milk, 1% milk fat
Cream, 10% milk fat (or use milk)
Butter
Sour cream, light
Cream cheese, light (5 1/3 oz or 83 g)
Cheddar cheese, light, shredded (1/2 cup)
Parmesan cheese, light, grated (optional for Pasta)
Blue cheese or feta

PRODUCE

Onion (1 1/2) for 2 meals
Red onion (1) for 2 meals
Sweet potato (1) (1 1/2 to 2 lbs or 675 to 900 g)
Cucumber (1/2)
Celery ribs (5) for 3 meals
Red bell pepper (1)
Green bell pepper (1/2)
Broccoli (1 head) & florets (1 1/2 lbs or 675 g)
Mushrooms (3)
Roma tomatoes (2) & Grape tomatoes (10)
Green leaf lettuce (1 head)
Salad greens (6 oz or 170 g)
Cantaloupe melon (1/4)
Cilantro (approx 1/4 cup)
Ceasar salad dressing, garlic lovers (1/2 cup)
  gourmet, refrigerated

BAKERY

Flour, multigrain or corn tortillas, 8" (6)
Multigrain buns (optional for Chili Macaroni Soup)

FROZEN FOODS

Baby peas (3 cups)

SPICES

Cayenne (optional for Donair-ish Wraps)
Chili powder
Cumin, ground
Garlic powder
Garlic and herb seasoning, salt-free
Italian seasoning
Onion powder
Original, all purpose seasoning, salt-free
Sesame seeds
Pepper

BAKING GOODS

Cooking spray & Olive oil, extra-virgin
Sesame oil
Vinegar & Balsamic vinegar
Sugar & Flour
Matchstick or slivered almonds

HELPERS

1 can diced tomatoes (28 fl oz or 796 mL)
Vegetable broth, reduced-sodium (3 1/2 to 4 cups)
Ranch dressing, fat-free
Mayonnaise, light
Dijon mustard
Liquid honey
Maple syrup
Soy sauce, reduced-sodium (or use Bragg)
Sweet Thai chili sauce (optional for Donairs)
Fish sauce
Hot wing sauce *I like Franks brand.*

DRY ESSENTIALS

Basmati rice (1 1/2 cups)
Wild and white rice (1 1/2 cups)
Macaroni pasta (2 cups)
Vermicelli pasta (12 oz or 340 g)
  (use regular vermicelli or spaghettini, only
  use rice vermicelli if wheat allergies in family)
Black-eyed peas (1/4 cup)
Chickpeas (1/4 cup)
Black beans (1/4 cup)
Orange & green lentils (2 Tbsp of each color)
Croutons (1/2 cup)

OTHER

Aluminum foil & Paper towels
Dubonnet (sweet red wine found in liquor store)
  or use red wine and a pinch of sugar

Custom Eat Sheet™

RECIPE NAME	Page
_____	
_____	
_____	
_____	
_____	

MEATS

DAIRY

PRODUCE

DRY ESSENTIALS

SPICES

BAKING GOODS

HELPERS

FROZEN FOODS

BAKERY

OTHER

RECIPE NAME   Page

MEATS

Chicken thighs, boneless, skinless (10-12)
  (1 3/4 lbs or 800 g)
Ground beef, extra-lean (2 lbs or 900 g) or turkey
Pork loin roast, boneless, trimmed
  (2-3 lbs or 900-1350 g)
Shrimp, large, cooked, peeled, deveined
  (1 lb or 450 g) or use a deli-roaster chicken

DAIRY

Butter
Eggs (2)
Milk, 1% milk fat
Cheddar cheese, light, shredded (1 cup)

PRODUCE

Fresh garlic (from a jar) or use cloves
Fresh ginger (from a jar) or fresh grated
Onion (1)
Red onion (1/8)
Green onion (1 bunch or 7-8)
Celery ribs (4)
Baby potatoes, red (20)
Mushrooms (8) *I prefer brown.*
Zucchini, medium (1)
Cucumber (1/4)
Red bell pepper (1) & Orange bell pepper (1/4)
Red chili pepper, small (1) (optional for Shrimp)
Sweet potato (1) (1 1/2 to 2 lbs or 675 g to 900 g)
Butternut squash (1) (2 to 2 1/2 lbs or 900 to 1125 g)
Snap peas (1 lb or 450 g)
Baby spinach, prewashed (6 oz or 170 g)
Coleslaw mix, fresh (1 lb or 450 g)
Cilantro (1/4 cup)
Lime (zest from 1/2)

DRY ESSENTIALS

Vermicelli pasta (12 oz or 340 g)
  (use regular vermicelli or spaghettini, only
  use rice vermicelli if wheat allergies in family)

OTHER

Aluminum foil

SPICES

Cayenne pepper (or use chipotle pepper)
Chili powder
Chipotle seasoning, salt-free
Cumin, ground
Garlic powder
Garlic and herb seasoning, salt-free
Ginger powder
Onion flakes
Orginal, all purpose seasoning, salt-free
Parsley, dried
Sesame seeds
Turmeric, ground
Salt & Pepper

BAKING GOODS

Cooking spray
Olive oil, extra-virgin
Sesame oil
Brown sugar
Matchstick almonds (optional for Coleslaw)

HELPERS

1 can coconut milk, light (14 fl oz or 400 mL)
Chicken broth, reduced-sodium (30 fl oz or 900 mL)
Peanut butter, light
Liquid honey
Salsa (mild, medium or hot) (3/4 cup)
Soy sauce, reduced-sodium (or use Bragg)
Curry paste (mild, madras or hot)
Fish sauce
Sweet Thai chili sauce
BBQ sauce (1 1/2 cup) for 2 meals
  (or use recipe on back flap)
Mayonnaise, light
Hot pepper relish or chopped up jalapenos (optional)
Salad dressing, light, your favorite (1/4 cup)
Coleslaw salad dressing (1/2 cup)

BAKERY

Breadcrumbs (1 1/2 cups)
Whole wheat buns (6)
Multigrain French loaf (1)

FROZEN FOODS

Stir-fry mixed vegetables (4 cups) (or fresh)
Sweet potato fries (1 lb or 450 g) (or regular fries)

Custom Eat Sheet™

RECIPE NAME   Page

_____

_____

_____

_____

_____

MEATS

DAIRY

PRODUCE

DRY ESSENTIALS

SPICES

BAKING GOODS

HELPERS

FROZEN FOODS

BAKERY

OTHER

MEATS

Sirloin or round roast, boneless, trimmed
  (5 lbs or 2250 g) Choose a thick roast. (for Raan
  Roast, Philly Cheese Steaks and a lunch)
Chicken wings, split (24) (approx 3 lbs or 1250 g)
Chicken breasts, boneless, skinless (3) (1 lb or 450 g)
Bacon bits, real (1/2 cup) for 2 meals

DAIRY

Milk, 1% milk fat
Butter
Cheddar cheese, sharp, light, shredded (1 cup)
Parmesan cheese, light, grated
Italian grated cheese blend (or mozzarella cheese,
  part-skim, shredded) (1/2 cup)

PRODUCE

Fresh garlic (from a jar) & Fresh ginger (from a jar)
Garlic cloves (4) or 2-3 tsp fresh (from a jar)
Baby potatoes (20) or 4 large
Onion (2) for 2 meals
English cucumber (1/2)
Tomato (1)
Red or orange bell pepper (1)
Green or red bell pepper (1)
Baby carrots (1 cup)
Cauliflower (1 cup)
Broccoli florets (1 lb or 225 g) for 2 meals
Green beans, fresh or frozen or 1 zucchini (1 cup)
Mushrooms (10)
Button mushrooms (15) or 8 mushrooms
Romaine lettuce (2 heads) for 2 meals

DRY ESSENTIALS

Croutons (1 cup) for 2 meals
Macaroni and cheese dinner (2 boxes,
  8 oz or 225 g each) *I like white cheddar.*
Vermicelli pasta (12 oz or 340 g)
  (use regular vermicelli, only use rice vermicelli
  if there are wheat allergies in your family)

FROZEN FOODS

Green beans, whole (1 lb or 450 g)

SPICES

Cardamom
Cinnamon, ground
Cloves, ground
Coriander
Cumin, ground
Garlic and herb seasoning, salt-free
Ginger, ground
Mustard powder
Onion powder
Original, all purpose seasoning, salt-free
Hot chili flakes (optional for General Tso)
Pepper

BAKING GOODS

Cooking spray
Sesame oil & Olive oil, extra-virgin
Balsamic vinegar
Rice vinegar
Cornstarch & Brown sugar
Peanuts, crushed (optional for General Tso)

HELPERS

1 can cream of mushroom soup, reduced-sodium
  (10 fl oz or 284 mL)
1 can solid tuna in water, no sodium
  (6 1/2 oz or 184 g) or canned or cooked chicken
Beef broth, reduced-sodium (2 cups)
Tomato paste (2 Tbsp)
Sambal Oelek (crushed chili paste)
Sweet Thai chili sauce
Hoisin sauce
Hot sauce
Worcestershire sauce
Soy sauce, reduced-sodium
Pickled jalapeño slices (optional for Caesar salad)
Sweet hot mustard
Mayonnaise, light
Ranch dressing, fat-free
Lemon juice
Maple syrup

BAKERY

Focaccia bread (optional for Wings)
Multigrain hot dog buns (4) or 2 sub buns

OTHER

Aluminum foil

Custom Eat Sheet™

RECIPE NAME   Page

_____

_____

_____

_____

_____

MEATS

DAIRY

PRODUCE

DRY ESSENTIALS

SPICES

BAKING GOODS

HELPERS

FROZEN FOODS

BAKERY

OTHER

MEATS

Roaster chicken, cooked from deli (2 cups)
  or use leftover chicken or pork or chicken breast
Chicken thighs, boneless, skinless (10-12)
  or 4-6 chicken breasts (1 3/4 lbs or 800 g)
Chicken breasts (2) (3/4 lb or 340 g)
Ground beef, extra lean (1 lb or 450 g)
Italian sausage meat, hot or mild (1 lb or 450 g)

DAIRY

Butter (optional)
Milk, 1% milk fat (optional for Beef Empanadas)
Sour cream, light
Parmesan cheese, light, grated (optional for
  Sicilian Penne Pasta)
Mozzarella, part-skim, shredded (1 cup)

PRODUCE

Fresh garlic (from a jar)
Onion (4) for 4 meals
Red onion (1/8)
Green onion (optional for BBQ Southwest Pizza)
Mushrooms (10)
Tomato (optional for BBQ Southwest Pizza)
Red bell pepper (2 1/4) for 3 meals
Green bell pepper (1) for 2 meals
Zucchini, small to medium (1)
Celery ribs (5) for 2 meals
Baby carrots (2 cups)
Carrots (2)
Cauliflower (1/4 head)
Broccoli florets (1 lb or 450 g)
Romaine lettuce (only 2 leaves)
  (or use green leaves from mixed salad greens)
Mixed salad greens, 1 bag (6 oz or 170 g)
Salad kit (optional for Chicken Tortellini Soup)
Cilantro, chopped (1/4 cup)
Papaya, small (or melon)
Cheese tortellini (4 cups) (in deli section)

DRY ESSENTIALS

Penne pasta (3 cups)
Basmati rice (1 1/2 cups)

SPICES

Basil leaves, dried (optional for Pasta)
Celery salt
Chili powder
Cinnamon, ground
Cloves, ground
Cumin, ground
Garlic & herb seasoning blend, salt-free
Hot chili flakes (optional for Pasta)
Italian seasoning
Mustard, dry
Oregano
Poultry seasoning
Pepper

BAKING GOODS

Olive oil, extra-virgin
Canola oil
White wine vinegar
Balsamic vinegar
Pumpkin seeds, raw

HELPERS

Chicken broth, reduced-sodium
  (3 3/4 - 4 1/4 cups) for 2 meals
Curried squash, carrot or pumpkin soup
  (16 fl oz or 500 mL) reserved from Curried
  Pumpkin Soup, pg. 72 or purchased
Southwest BBQ sauce
Worcestershire sauce
Hot sauce (optional for Chicken Tortellini Soup)
Chunky salsa (mild, medium or hot)
  (2 1/2 - 3 cups) for 3 meals
Ranch dressing, fat-free (optional for BBQ Pizza)
Honey, liquid or softened
Maple syrup

FROZEN FOODS

Puff pastry, 1 sheet (8 oz or 225 g) or use block
Mixed veggies (1 cup) (optional for Soup)

BAKERY

12" thin crust pizza base (1/2 lb or 225 g)

OTHER

Aperitif wine (Dubonnet) or sweet sherry
  (found in liquor store)
Paper towel (optional)

Custom Eat Sheet™

RECIPE NAME   Page

_____

_____

_____

_____

_____

MEATS

DAIRY

PRODUCE

DRY ESSENTIALS

SPICES

BAKING GOODS

HELPERS

FROZEN FOODS

BAKERY

OTHER

MEATS

Chicken thighs, boneless, skinless
  (1 1/2 lbs or 675 g)
Ground beef, extra-lean (1 1/2 lbs or 675 g)
Pork loin chops, 1/2" thick, boneless, trimmed (4)
  (1 1/2 lbs or 675 g)
Bacon strips, fully cooked bacon, low-sodium (7)
Salmon filets, boneless, skinless (4-6)
  or butterflied chicken (1 1/2 lbs or 675 g)

DAIRY

Pillsbury Crescent Rolls (1 pkg) (8 oz or 225 g)
Butter
Sour cream, light (optional for Tamale Pie)
Vanilla yogurt, low-fat (optional for Fruit Salad)
Cheddar cheese, light, shredded (1 cup)
Parmesan cheese, light, grated (optional for Pasta)

PRODUCE

Fresh garlic (from a jar)
Garlic cloves (5) (or from a jar)
Shallots (1-2)
Onion (1)
Red onion (1/4)
Green onion (2) (optional for Lemongrass Chicken)
Baby potatoes (20) or 4 large, thin skin
Broccoli florets (1 lb or 450 g)
Asparagus (20) (1 lb or 450 g)
Green bell pepper (1/2)
Thai chilies, red (2-3)
Lemongrass stalks (2)
Fennel root bulb (1) for 2 meals
  (also called anise)
Mandarin orange (1)
Cantaloupe or honey dew melon (2 cups)
Berries (blackberries etc.) (3/4 cup)
Strawberries (1 cup)
Green grapes, seedless (1 cup)

SPICES

Chili powder
Curry powder
Garlic and herb seasoning, salt-free
Hot chili flakes
Italian seasoning
Oregano leaves
Original, all purpose seasoning, salt-free
Pepper

BAKING GOODS

Cooking spray
Olive oil, extra virgin
Canola oil (or peanut oil)
Sugar
Raisins
Peanuts (optional for Lemongrass Chicken)

HELPERS

1 can Italian stewed tomatoes (28 fl oz or 796 mL)
Dijon mustard
Fish sauce
Basil pesto (1/4 cup) (found near pasta sauces)
Salsa (mild, medium or hot) (1 1/2 cups)
  (+ optional for Tamale Pie)

FROZEN FOODS

Corn (1 cup)
Green beans (1 lb or 450 g)
Baby peas (3 cups)

DRY ESSENTIALS

Basmati rice (1 1/2 cups)
Mixed rice, white and wild (1 1/2 cups)
  I like Canoe brand.
Penne pasta (3 1/2 cups)
Croutons (optional for Pasta)
Panko flakes (1/4 cup) (found near coating mixes)

OTHER

Paper towels

Custom Eat Sheet™

RECIPE NAME   Page

_____
_____
_____
_____
_____

MEATS

DAIRY

PRODUCE

DRY ESSENTIALS

SPICES

BAKING GOODS

HELPERS

FROZEN FOODS

BAKERY

OTHER

MEATS

Chicken breasts, boneless, skinless (3) (1 lb or 450 g)
Chicken thighs, boneless, skinless (10-12)
  (1 3/4 lb or 800 g)
Ground beef, extra-lean (1 lb or 450 g)
Ham, boneless, ready to serve, reduced-sodium
  (3-4 lbs or 1.3-1.8 kg)
Shrimp, peeled, deveined, frozen or fresh
  (1/2 lb or 225 g)
Scallops, frozen or fresh (1 lb or 450 g)

DAIRY

Butter
Milk, 1% milk fat (1 cup) for 2 meals
Cream, 10% milk fat (1/2 cup)
Egg (1)
Sharp cheddar cheese, light, grated (1/2 cup)
Feta cheese, light or goat cheese (1/4 cup)
Mozzarella or gruyere cheese (optional for Coquille)
Mascarpone cheese (1/2 cup)

PRODUCE

Fresh garlic (from a jar) & Garlic bulb (1)
Onion (3) for 3 meals
Green onions (4)
Red onion (1/8)
Celery ribs (2)
Green bell pepper (1)
Red bell pepper (1)
Mushrooms (28) (for 3 meals)
Broccoli florets (1 lb or 450 g)
Potatoes, Yukon Gold
  (2 lbs or 900 g) or 6 thin skin potatoes
Baby spinach, prewashed (1 bag) (6 oz or 170 g)

DRY ESSENTIALS

Basmati rice (1 1/2 cups)
Vermicelli pasta (12 oz or 340 g)
  (use regular vermicelli, only use rice vermicelli
  if there are wheat allergies in your family)

BAKERY

Fresh buns or foccacia (optional for Soup)

SPICES

Bay leaves (3)
Curry powder
Hot chili flakes (optional for 2 meals)
Italian seasoning
Mustard, dry (1/4 cup)
Paprika, smoked (optional for Spinach Salad)
Parsley, dried
Salt & Pepper

BAKING GOODS

Olive oil, extra virgin & Canola oil
Vinegar
Balsamic vinegar (or use bottled dressing)
Cornstarch
Flour
Sugar & Brown sugar
Cashews, unsalted or lightly salted (1/3 cup)
Pecan pieces (optional for Spinach Salad)

HELPERS

1 can Italian or chili stewed tomatoes
  (14 fl oz or 400 mL)
1 can pasta sauce (choose a lower sodium brand)
  (24 fl oz or 680 mL) or reserved 3 cups of
  sauce from Calabrese Lasagna
1 can consommé (10 fl oz or 284 g)
1 can chicken broth, reduced-sodium
  (10 fl oz or 284 mL)
Ketchup
Dijon mustard
Salsa (mild, medium or hot) (1/2 cup)
Hot chili sauce (optional for Cashew Chicken)
Maple syrup

FROZEN FOODS

Baby peas (3 cups)
Mixed veggies (3 cups)
Blueberries, wild (1/2 cup)
Puff pastry patty shells (1 package of 6)
  (10 oz or 300 g)

OTHER

Aluminum foil & Paper towel
White wine (1/2 cup)
Aperitif red wine or Marsala wine or port
  (1/2 cup) *I like Dubonnet* (found in a liquor store)

Custom Eat Sheet™

RECIPE NAME   Page

_____

_____

_____

_____

_____

MEATS

DAIRY

PRODUCE

DRY ESSENTIALS

SPICES

BAKING GOODS

HELPERS

FROZEN FOODS

BAKERY

OTHER

RECIPE NAME · Page

MEATS

Roaster chicken precooked from deli (2 lbs / 900 g)
Chicken cutlets or butterflied chicken breasts (4)
  (1 1/3 lbs or 600 g)
Chicken breasts (2) (optional for Tarts)
Ground lamb or beef (1 lb or 450 g)

DAIRY

Butter
Milk, 1% milk fat (1 cup)
Eggs (3) for 2 meals
Brie or cambozola cheese (4 oz or 125 g)
Cambozola cheese or cream cheese (1 1/2 Tbsp)
  (for Chicken Burgers)
Goat cheese or feta cheese, light (1/4 cup)

PRODUCE

Fresh garlic (from a jar) for 2 meals or use cloves
Onions (3) for 2 meals
Red onion (1/2) for 2 meals
Onion, sweet white, large (1)
Green onions (4)
Cherry tomatoes (8-12)
Tomatoes (2)
Mushrooms (10)
Potatoes, thin skin or baby potatoes (2 lbs or 900 g)
Cucumber, English (1)
Celery ribs (2)
Baby carrots (1 lb or 450 g)
Peas, snap (1 1/2 lbs or 675 g) for 3 meals
Asparagus spears (20) (1 lb or 450 g)
Mint leaves (10) (+ extra for garnish)
Cilantro, chopped (1/4 - 1/2 cup)
Lettuce leaves (2 cups)
Mixed salad greens, 1 bag (6 oz or 170 g)
Pears (1-2)
Raspberries (1/2 cup)

DRY ESSENTIALS

Basmati rice (1 1/2 cup)
Panko flakes (1 cup) (found near coating mixes)
  or use cornflake crumbs

SPICES

Cayenne or chipotle pepper (optional for Burgers)
Oregano
Parsley, dried
Pepper

BAKING GOODS

Cooking spray & Canola oil
Olive oil, extra-virgin & Sesame oil
Balsamic vinegar
Brown sugar
Flour (if using pastry blocks for Tarts)
Raisins (1/2 cup)
Matchstick almonds (1/4 cup)
Pecans (optional for Snap Pea Salad)

HELPERS

2 cans tuna, salmon or crab, in water
  (6 1/2 or 184 g each)
1 can cream of mushroom soup, reduced-sodium
  (10 fl oz or 284 mL)
1 jar green pimento olives or any pitted olives of
  your choice, sliced (1/3 cup)
Mayonnaise, light
Dijon mustard
Worcestershire sauce
Sweet Thai chili sauce
Vidalia salad dressing, onion, light (1/3 cup)
  (or your favorite dressing)
Ranch dressing, light (optional for Veggies)
Maple syrup (optional for pecans for Pea Salad)
Mint jelly or mango chutney (optional for Meatballs)
Red pepper jelly (found near gourmet condiments)
  (or apple jelly)
Lime juice

FROZEN FOODS

Green beans (4 cups)
Puff pastry (2 sheets) (16 oz or 450 g)
  (or 2 puff pastry blocks)

BAKERY

Whole wheat bread (6 slices)
Hamburger buns, multigrain (4-6)

OTHER

Paper towel
Waxed paper
Large plastic resealable bag

Custom Eat Sheet™

RECIPE NAME   Page

_____

_____

_____

_____

_____

MEATS

DAIRY

PRODUCE

DRY ESSENTIALS

SPICES

BAKING GOODS

HELPERS

FROZEN FOODS

BAKERY

OTHER

MEATS

Chicken breasts, boneless, skinless (7)
  (2 1/2 lbs or 1135 g) for 2 meals
Italian sausage, hot or mild (1/4 cup)
Ground beef, extra-lean or chicken (1 lb or 450 g)
Flank or skirt steak (1 1/2 lbs or 675 g)
Bacon bits (optional for Caesar Salad)
Shrimp, peeled and deveined (1 lb or 450 g)

DAIRY

Milk, 1% milk fat (3/4 cup)
Egg (1)
Sour cream, light (optional for Yams)
Ricotta cheese or 1% cottage cheese (1 cup)
Mozzarella cheese, part-skim, shredded (1 cup)
Parmesan cheese, light, grated

PRODUCE

Onions (2 1/2) for 2 meals
Green onion (4) (+ optional for Yams)
Red onion (1/8)
Lemongrass stalks (2) (or in a tube)
Red Thai chilies, small (3)
Red bell pepper (1/2)
Celery ribs (4) for 2 meals
Mushrooms (16) for 2 meals
  I prefer brown but you can use white.
Baby carrots (2 cups)
  (or 4 sliced in half lengthwise)
Carrots (3) for 2 meals
Broccoli florets
  (2 1/4 lbs or 1 kg) for 3 meals
Beets (3)
Yams, long, skinny (6) (1 1/2-2 lbs or 675-900 g)
  (or large sweet potato, see recipe instructions)
Potatoes, thin skin (4) (2 lbs or 900 g)
Romaine lettuce (1 head)
Mixed salad greens, 1 bag (6 oz or 170 g)
Cilantro (1/4 cup)
Tofu, pressed (6 oz or 170 g)

SPICES

Five spice powder
Garlic and herb seasoning, salt-free
Garlic powder
Hot chili flakes (optional for Flank Steak)
Italian seasoning
Kaffir lime leaves (4) (or 4 bay leaves & lime zest)
Lemon pepper, salt-free
Pepper

BAKING GOODS

Olive oil, extra-virgin
Canola oil
Sesame oil
Balsamic vinegar
Flour
Brown sugar

HELPERS

1 can tomato pasta sauce, choose a
  lower-sodium brand (24 fl oz or 680 mL)
1 can cream of celery soup or use cream of
  chicken (10 fl oz or 284 mL)
Vinaigrette dressing, fat-free (1/4 cup)
Caesar dressing, fat-free or light (1/3 cup)
Fish sauce
Lime juice (1/4 cup) (+ lime zest if using bay leaves)
Tom Yum paste (hot and sour paste)
Cherry or raspberry jam

DRY ESSENTIALS

Spaghetti pasta (8 oz or 225 g)
Vermicelli pasta (6 oz or 170 g)
  (use regular vermicelli or spaghettini, only
  use rice vermicelli if wheat allergies in family)
Croutons (1/2 cup)
Panko flakes (1 cup) (found near coating mixes)

FROZEN FOODS

Puff pastry (1 sheet) (8 oz or 225 g) or use a block
Mixed veggies (1 cup)

OTHER

Aluminum foil & Plastic wrap
Waxed paper
Red aperitif wine
  I use Dubonnet (found in a liquor store)

Custom Eat Sheet™

RECIPE NAME   Page

_____

_____

_____

_____

_____

MEATS

DAIRY

PRODUCE

DRY ESSENTIALS

SPICES

BAKING GOODS

HELPERS

FROZEN FOODS

BAKERY

OTHER

MEATS

Chicken breasts w/ skin, bone in (4)
  (1 3/4 lb or 800 g)
Chicken breasts, boneless, skinless (3)
  (1 lb or 450 g) or use sausage meat for Perogies
Sirloin steak, trimmed, 1 1/2" to 2" thick
  (1 1/2 lbs or 675 g)
Ham, cooked, low-sodium (1/2 lb or 225 g ham
  steak) or use reserved from Baked Ham pg.114
Canadian back bacon (6 slices) (6 oz or 170 g)
Scallops (1 lb or 450 g) The larger ones have
  better flavor, so avoid the real tiny ones.

DAIRY

Butter
Milk, 1% milk fat (2 1/2 cups)
Sour cream, light (1/2 cup)
Eggs (6)
Cheddar cheese, light, shredded (2 cups)
Feta cheese, light, crumbled (1/2 cup)
Goat cheese or feta, light, crumbled (1/4 cup)

PRODUCE

Fresh garlic (from a jar) & Garlic clove (1)
Shallot (1) or 3 green onions
Onion (1 1/2) for 2 meals
Red onion (1/2) for 2 meals
Green onions (2-3)
Green bell pepper (1 1/4) for 2 meals
Red bell pepper (1/4)
English cucumber (1/2)
Zucchini (2) for 2 meals
Asparagus spears (27) (1 1/3 lb or 600 g) for 2
  meals (or replace 7 with broccoli florets for Strata)
Roma tomatoes (4) for 2 meals
Mushrooms (18) for 2 meals
Corn on the cob (2) or 4 small
Baby potatoes (20) or 4 large potatoes
Romaine lettuce, shredded (1/2 cup)
Baby spinach, prewashed (6 oz or 170 g)
Mango (1)
Spartan apples (2)

SPICES

Chipotle pepper
Hot pepper seasoning (such as Club House Hot
  Shot or any hot pepper blend)
Lemon pepper, salt-free
Mustard, dry
Oregano leaves
Original, all purpose seasoning, salt-free
Sage leaves
S.W. chipotle seasoning, salt-free
Thyme leaves
Salt & Pepper

BAKING GOODS

Cooking spray & Olive oil, extra-virgin
Red wine vinegar or balsamic vinegar
Nuts (such as pecans) (optional for Spinach Salad)

HELPERS

Black olives (optional for Greek Salad)
Mayonnaise, light (1/4 cup)
Chunky salsa (mild, medium or hot) (1 cup)
Hot pepper sauce
Soy sauce, reduced-sodium
Vinaigrette dressing, fat-free (1/4 cup)
Basil pesto (found near pasta sauces)
Tomato or basil pesto (used for Steak Sandwich)
Fig jam or peach preserve
Lemon juice
Apple juice, unsweetened (1 1/3 cup)

FROZEN FOODS

Perogies (20) (1 1/3 lb or 600 g)
  We use potato and onion perogies.

DRY ESSENTIALS

Basmati rice (1 1/2 cups)
Tortilla chips (1/4 cup)

BAKERY

French loaf
Dried bread cubes, whole wheat (5 cups)
  (found in Bakery section near large bread crumbs)

OTHER

Aluminum foil
Paper towels

INDEXES

Main Component

beef, chicken, pork, seafood, vegetarian

'cause you have an idea
of what you'd like

Prep Code

by color
for when timing is everything

Fat Content

from lowest to highest

'cause your health requires you
to watch your fat intake

Index by Main Component

Index by Main Component

Index By Prep Code

Index By Fat Content

Do You Ever Wonder Who Our Test Families Are?

They are people like you who inspire us to do what we do! They take the time out of their busy days to email us and tell us how our work has impacted their relationships and dinners at home! They are people who THANK US?—for letting them test our new creations and give us their feedback! WOW!!
They are genuine and have taken their health seriously! They are the kind of people who take action! They are the kind of people who have common sense and get it that it's all about balance! They are people who know that when they test our food, they are helping thousands of families get back to the dinner table! They see the bigger picture! They are blatantly honest and point out all of our errors so that the recipes and books over all will be the best they can be! They make us cry (happy tears) and they make us laugh! There have been times we laughed so hard….like when one test family pointed out a few things like…Cashew Chicken: "I didn't know what type of cashews to buy. I wanted to buy a roasted cashew but they were all salted. Instead I bought a baking cashew. They looked like a bunch of pale British sunbathers on a vermicelli beach!" Oooorrrr…"I was surprised by the vast amount of baby spinach needed. I found that the common size for bags of baby spinach was 170 g, so I didn't know whether to buy two bags or a giant box-o-spinach, which was about 450 g and seemed enough to feed a herd of goats for about a week!" It got to the point where Valerie would announce to the office…Karen sent new feedback!!!!…We would all run over to her desk so we could have our belly laugh for the day! SOOOOO, NO FAMILIES…IT'S US WHO NEEDS TO THANK YOU!!! Our test families for this book are…

The Bass family, The Bayne family, The Bond family, The Burke family, The Collyer family, The Colwell family, The Currie family, The Dorey family, The Douglas family, The Follows family, The Gartner family, The Gillis family, The Hanson family, The Hebert family, The Johnston family, The Langlois-Lott family, The Lavoie family, The Leis family, The Lilly family, The Mantyak family, The McCallum family, The Mercer family, The Molde family, The Morley family, The Reid family, The Sandy family, The Schermann Norris family, The Scott family, The Shaw family, The Strand family, The Suriano family and The Wuthrich family!

After testing—then thanks to these guys…retesting…here are some things they had to say about the meals in this book!

Mole Chicken: To be honest, I was a little freaked out about this one (I thought the ingredients were a little out there), but I was shocked to see my two year old cramming the chicken in her mouth!

Calabrese Lasagna: A great weekday rush version of lasagna! I love that I have a back up meal in the meantime!

Crispy Lemon Chicken With Rice: Super tasty! Lemon sauce was just like the take-out kind!

Raspberry-Maple Ribs: I loved using the slow cooker, they turned out amazing and dinner was done so fast!

Sticky Sesame Chicken Drumsticks: The kids could not get enough of this – they want it every day!

Chicken Caesar Pasta with Peas: Even our picky eater loved this!

Buffalo Salmon: I never cook salmon because it is not a favorite of my husband or mine but this was delicious!

Pulled Pork on a Bun: I love this slow cooker version – so easy! The Mexi-Mayo is great!

Shrimp Toss in a Coconut Broth: Delish and looks beautiful!

Curried Butternut Squash Soup: Very easy to prepare and a very quick dinner!

Peanut Butter and Honey Chicken: Yum yum! The kids loved it and my husband said it was delicious!

Raan (sort of) with Onion Jam: Delicious! The onion jam was amazing and beef turned out great.

Tuna Macaroni Bake: My 4 1/2 year old asked, "Can we eat this every day? Even for breakfast??"

Philly Cheese Steaks: The idea of using hot dog buns is brilliant and to be able to use leftover beef makes it so easy!

General Tso's Chicken: Loved by my kids and eaten with no extra encouragement! 6 1/2 year old, "tasty and yummy!" 4 1/2 year old, "yuhhhh-ummm!"

Chicken Tortellini Soup: Absolutely loved this soup! Great updated twist on the boring chicken noodle soup.

Beef Empanadas: Excellent! We loved it. I never thought I'd be able to make these.

Chili Glazed Chicken: The little kids liked it even more than the adults did! Even the VERY picky eater!

Sicilian Penne Pasta: My husband (who doesn't usually like to try new things) liked this enough to have seconds! Wasn't too sure when I saw the ingredients but was very surprised, even the 5 year old ate it.

BBQ Southwest Pizza: The flavor was phenomenal! I think now my hubby is comparing every recipe to this one!

Lemongrass Chicken: Was hard to convince hubby to try lemongrass, but success! My husband doesn't ever like curry – but something about this – he'd definitely eat it again.

Salmon with Mandarins: Again another wonderful salmon recipe that is getting me hooked on fish!

Tamale Pie: At first when I had to 'caramelize' the onions I thought, "Ooh, I don't know if I like how long this will take!" but the rest of the recipe is so EASY! Yum yum yum!! This one is so good that you have to be careful about portion sizes – very easy to overeat! This was a "go to bed and dream about it" recipe.

Pesto Dijon Pork Chops: Absolute hit! Can't wait to make it again. I think this sauce is my new favorite. Just amazing.

Baked Ham with Hot Sweet Mustard: I always think of ham as a Sunday night dinner thing, but this was very easy to cook and it was a wonderful change for a weeknight meal!

Coquille St. Jacques: For this meal I even took the extra time to plate it properly, filling it with the seafood mixture and placing the pastry shell top at a nice angle on top of it. It felt like fine dining – until my husband picked it up like a hamburger and ate it. Liked using raw shrimp; it tasted so fresh when cooked. Easy, elegant meal.

Cheeseburger Soup: For the small amount of prep time, I must admit that it was a real treat to come home to a fully prepared meal. I think I will absolutely love this meal on a cold winter's day. I really appreciated the fact that it didn't taste like a slow cooker meal. So easy to make; nice to smell a meal cooking when walking in the door; smells great. Reluctant eaters enjoyed it as well.

Mediterranean Chicken: Very flavorful and super easy too!

Pear, Brie and Caramelized Onion Tart: I was surprised at how much I enjoyed this particular meal. This was easy to cook up. To be honest, I would never have tried this recipe if we weren't a test family!

Lamb Meatballs: Everyone really enjoyed this one. It was just so easy to whip up!

Tuna (or Salmon or Crab) Cakes: As a family we don't really like tuna, but the use of lime juice, cilantro and sweet chili really made this recipe!

Spicy Crispy Chicken Burgers: The use of camobozola cheese and red pepper jelly was a unique and unforgettable flavor!

Baked Spaghetti & Meatballs: Loved it, easy to prepare and very kid friendly.

Grilled Flank Steak: MMMMMMMM (My father is a man of few words, that was his sound while eating, you know it was good!) The flavor combination of the marinated steak with the yams was amazing! Would never have put those ingredients together for the marinade. Was very flavorful and the color was very appealing!

Chicken Pot Pie: Very good! A hit with everyone! Very good, quick and easy!

Roasted Fig and Pesto Chicken: Can't wait to have it again, absolutely loved it. I couldn't get over the AROMA this recipe had. I heard the sizzling and had to look through the glass, it tastes as good as it sounds and smells. Absolute hit with us!

Ham Strata: I loved that I could make this the night before and have it all ready to pop in the oven. It's like getting out of making dinner for the night!

Chicken Fajita Perogies: To die for! Can't wait to have again!

Steak Sandwich: One of the best sandwiches I've ever had. The chipotle mayo was to die for!

Smoked Canadian Bacon, Scallops, Apples, Zucchini: A lovely mixture of sweet and smoky! Delicious and easy!

Our Team

God - no picture on file
Well God—you did it again! You kept us excited about helping families get back to the dinner table, despite our crazy busy schedule! Thank you for believing in me and trusting that I will serve well! I don't know what I would do if you were not part of our team!

Photography - Lisa Fryklund
Lisa is with us once again and once again we are astounded with how she manages to make real food (not food styled) look so great! She has become a trusted member of our team and a dear friend! We love you Lis! Lisa is a photographer and an award winning cinematographer with a wide range of experience. She has travelled the world filming for Discovery, TLC, CBC, ABC, History, CMT, HGTV and National Geographic. Lisa Fryklund is the owner of her own company. **Fryklund Cinematography**   **www.fryklund.com**

Illustrations - Hermann Brandt
Hermann joins us once again and as always he is a sheer joy to work with! He is talented, his work is always on time and he is an all around nice guy! We're very blessed to have you on our team Hermann! Hermann studied art at the Pretoria Technicon Arts School in South Africa and is the owner of his own company.
Clear Air Art Studio   **http://clearairartstudio.blogspot.com**

Food Photography Support - Solange Adams
One person I can always count on to help on our photo shoots is my amazing, mother-in-law, Solange. She gets right in there, picking all the right plates and accessories. She's got a special eye for what makes food look great! I guess that makes sense seeing she is such an amazing cook and certainly knows her way around a kitchen. What would we do without you?

Special Advisors - Murray Smith, Kent Emmons, Scott Fry
Many years ago my beautiful son, Doug, threw open the door after school as he often did! But this time as he bounced by me on his way to his bedroom to unload his books he quipped, "Today my teacher said…It's funny how the busiest people always seem to have the time…that's like you mom!" Unbeknownst to him, my tears began to well—knowing that my beautiful son thought I deserved to be in such a category! Here are three other people that fit this category to a tee! Murray Smith, **www.accessmainstreet.com**, Kent Emmons, **www.kentdirect.com** and Scott Fry, **www.radicalaxis.com** (owner of one of the world's most cutting edge animation companies). Through the process of content and design, they were all just a click away, even though they are some of the busiest people I have ever met in my life! We will never forget your kindness, your passion, your time and I believe I can say your friendship!

Our Team

Graphic Design/Marketing/Office Comedian - Megan Sellar
Megan joined our team this year and brought with her a wide range of talents! She is quick as a whip, has a smile that can compete, full on, with the sun and can have us all in hysterics, without even trying! What a joy it has been to work with you, Megan. I know that no matter what life brings you, you will do very well!

You can reach Megan at **misellar@gmail.com**

Graphic Support - Kris Nielson
Kris joins our team once again and is such a lovely person to be around. We are very blessed to have you right at our doorstep to guide us through set up and iron out our glitches! Kris is an international award winning graphic artist as well as a publisher author, photographer and a certified outdoor instructor and guide.

Kris Nielson Design   **www.krisdesign.ca**

Assistant and Research - Valerie Friesen
Valerie joined our team this summer before heading back to university! She is a nutritionist who loves food almost as much as I do! Valerie mulled over pages upon pages of editing, research and anything else we dished her (pun intended). We feel very blessed that we got to spend the summer with you Valerie and hope your studies give you great joy as you bring your food knowledge to every corner of the world!

Writer - Summer Felix
Summer joined our team this year to help out with the writing. It was the first time I had ever done that…and what a treat! I would send her dictations… with my hands flapping with my over excitable (and sometimes annoying) rants…and she magically condensed it all for us to make editing soooooo much easier! Summer also has helped write a show I did in the U.S. so I'm sure we will be working together for many years to come!

You can reach Summer at **summerfelix@yahoo.com**

Dietitian, Diabetes Consultant - Sandra Burgess B.A.Sc.,R.D.,C.D.E.
Sandra joins us once again to convert all our nutritional data to U.S. and Canadian diabetes food exchange and food group values. She has been an invaluable member of our team and we feel very blessed to have her on board once again! Sandra is an avid volunteer with the Canadian Diabetes Association, Inn from the Cold Society and the very famous Calgary Stampede. She is a registered dietitian and certified diabetes educator with over 30 years of experience.

Obsessed With Food

Yeeeeeah!!!!! After 8 months without a break, there we were in Palm Springs! As Ron and I held hands and smiled at each other we both knew our minds were in sync…the week would include relaxing by the pool, reading books we never get to read—in long sessions that is—(we do read them page by page as we sit on the throne ooooor in the car…I drive, Ron reads!) We would take tennis lessons and go for bike rides! And we made a pact, no talking business the whole time we were away!

Our room had a complete kitchen so the first day we decided to take a bike ride to the grocery store and pick up groceries for the week. Once at the store we were like two little kids in a candy shop! We squealed over all the wonderful dishes we would make with all our new finds! I guess we should have known something was up when the butcher kept laughing as he passed by! Juuust a minute…how many times has he passed by? What time is it? How is it possible that we were swooning over food for more than four hours! On our ride back we came across lemon trees…right on the boulevard!!! Who could resist?

We parked our bikes; Ron scaled the tree and shook down as many lemons as I could gather! Homemade lemonade with lemons from the boulevard…what could be more exciting than that? I mean really!! We walked in the door and immediately began fixing a fabulous new dinner creation! We arrived at the pool just as the sun was setting!

The next day, we decided to try biking again! Off we went with anticipation of where we would go…and there it was, a second hand bookstore! We were amidst famous authors who paved the way for all of us creative numbskulls. I, I, I mean geniuses! We love the smell of old books, in fact we are amazed that no one has created an "old book" deodorizer! What? I'd buy it! There we were sitting…for hours in the…you got it, cookbook section! (Don't laugh, I did manage to walk away with one of Julia Child's originals!) We arrived back at the pool, once again, too dark to read…then realized something magical! We can't go away and not talk about business, because we are obsessed with food! We love talking about it, shopping for it, cooking it, eating it, reading about it and helping people with it! That holiday put us in a place of peace we had never been before! We understood for the first time, how fortunate we are that we look forward to working on our business rather than having to work on our business (whether on holidays or not)! Now how blessed is that?

Sandi

My Books

What you can count on!

The same platform, so no matter what book you use you get the same benefits.

The platform for all books

Six times tested and retested by real families on the go in real life. Each meal takes no longer than 20 minutes to prepare, is color coded for speed, and follows basic balanced eating, rather than diet fads. Each portion is a proper serving size, is limited to **approx 500 calories for the whole meal** with a few exceptions and follows healthy guidelines on fat, carbs and sodium. You make each meal by starting at the top and working your way down, reading left to right, just as you would a book. Our trademark format means less confusion during weekday cooking. Clocks indicate prep time and we even tell you when dinner is ready. Color photos of real food with no photography tricks. Equipment lists and coinciding Eat Sheets™ (grocery lists) for each week so that you are ready for the grocery store.

What makes each book different?

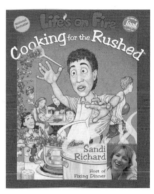

Life's on Fire

This was my very first book. I wanted people to know that dinner could be easy, lip smacking delicious and healthy all while meeting their weekday needs for speed! *Life's on Fire* has 10 full weeks of nutritionally balanced dinners with corresponding Eat Sheets™.

The Healthy Family

Helps our readers sift through the mounds of health information in the most simplified and fun way possible! Packed with advice from Dr. Kelly Brett and Dr. George Lambrose as well as a big thumbs up from Dr. Gordon Matheson M.D. PhD. from Stanford University, this book took complex information on the energy balance between food and activity and made it all very easy to understand. It's a fun, informative and provocative read! *The Healthy Family* has 7 full weeks of nutritionally balanced dinners with corresponding Eat Sheets™.

The (Family) Dinner Fix

I understand that our readers are becoming more sophisticated, as families in North America adopt the many different cultural foods our beautiful countries have to offer. With this in mind, I've taken work-week favorites and created 10 weeks of amazing dinners with corresponding Eat Sheets™.

Dinner Survival

Takes a good look at the complexities of today's ever changing family. It offers tips and tricks to help you to get dinner to the table effortlessly. Everything from how to cook the perfect steak to "Why didn't my slow cooker recipe work?" Many of the meals were created for real families featured on my show *Fixing Dinner* on Food Network Canada, American Life and Discovery Asia. *Dinner Survival* has 10 weeks of amazing dinners with corresponding Eat Sheets™.

DINNER CAN BE EASY!

Love dinner while improving your **health**, **budget** and **relationships**!

Sandi has an **Eating Forward**™ program for your organization, agency or corporation.

Why not **fundraise** with a program that brings families back to the dinner table...and promotes healthy eating on a budget?

Online free printable Eat Sheets™ for all books.

www.eatingforward.com

    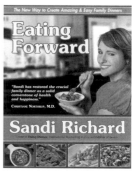

NEW! Eat Sheet™ Generator

What is an Eat Sheet™ Generator?

It's software that allows you to choose dinners from any of Sandi's books, then print the grocery list.

<u>Create your perfect dinner week!</u>
1- Choose your favorite meals from any of Sandi's books
2- Print your own customized **Eat Sheet**™

Watch for Sandi's new membersite!
www.eatingforward.com!